Smart Machines
Complete Self-Assessment Guide

The guidance in this Self-Assessment is based
practices and standards in business process ar
quality management. The guidance is also based on the professional
judgment of the individual collaborators listed in the Acknowledgments.

Table of Contents

About The Art of Service

The Art of Service, Business Process Architects since 2000, is dedicated to helping stakeholders achieve excellence.

Defining, designing, creating, and implementing a process to solve a stakeholders challenge or meet an objective is the most valuable role… In EVERY group, company, organization and department.

Unless you're talking a one-time, single-use project, there should be a process. Whether that process is managed and implemented by humans, AI, or a combination of the two, it needs to be designed by someone with a complex enough perspective to ask the right questions.

Someone capable of asking the right questions and step back and say, 'What are we really trying to accomplish here? And is there a different way to look at it?'

With The Art of Service's Standard Requirements Self-Assessments, we empower people who can do just that — whether their title is marketer, entrepreneur, manager, salesperson, consultant, Business Process Manager, executive assistant, IT Manager, CIO etc... —they are the people who rule the future. They are people who watch the process as it happens, and ask the right questions to make the process work better.

Contact us when you need any support with this Self-Assessment and any help with templates, blue-prints and examples of standard documents you might need:

http://theartofservice.com
service@theartofservice.com

Acknowledgments

This checklist was developed under the auspices of The Art of Service, chaired by Gerardus Blokdyk.

Representatives from several client companies participated in the preparation of this Self-Assessment.

In addition, we are thankful for the design and printing services provided.

Included Resources - how to access

Included with your purchase of the book is the Smart Machines Self-Assessment Spreadsheet Dashboard which contains all questions and Self-Assessment areas and auto-generates insights, graphs, and project RACI planning - all with examples to get you started right away.

How? Simply send an email to
access@theartofservice.com
with this books' title in the subject to get the Smart Machines Self Assessment Tool right away.

You will receive the following contents with New and Updated specific criteria:

•	The latest quick edition of the book in PDF

•	The latest complete edition of the book in PDF, which criteria correspond to the criteria in...

•	The Self-Assessment Excel Dashboard, and...

•	Example pre-filled Self-Assessment Excel Dashboard to get familiar with results generation

•	In-depth specific Checklists covering the topic

•	Project management checklists and templates to assist with implementation

INCLUDES LIFETIME SELF ASSESSMENT UPDATES

Every self assessment comes with Lifetime Updates and Lifetime Free Updated Books. Lifetime Updates is an industry-first feature which allows you to receive verified self assessment updates, ensuring you always have the most accurate information at your fingertips.

Get it now- you will be glad you did - do it now, before you forget.

Send an email to **access@theartofservice.com** with this books' title in the subject to get the Smart Machines Self Assessment Tool right away.

Your feedback is invaluable to us

If you recently bought this book, we would love to hear from you! You can do this by writing a review on amazon (or the online store where you purchased this book) about your last purchase! As part of our continual service improvement process, we love to hear real client experiences and feedback.

How does it work?
To post a review on Amazon, just log in to your account and click on the Create Your Own Review button (under Customer Reviews) of the relevant product page. You can find examples of product reviews in Amazon. If you purchased from another online store, simply follow their procedures.

What happens when I submit my review?
Once you have submitted your review, send us an email at review@theartofservice.com with the link to your review so we can properly thank you for your feedback.

Purpose of this Self-Assessment

This Self-Assessment has been developed to improve understanding of the requirements and elements of Smart Machines, based on best practices and standards in business process architecture, design and quality management.

It is designed to allow for a rapid Self-Assessment to determine how closely existing management practices and procedures correspond to the elements of the Self-Assessment.

The criteria of requirements and elements of Smart Machines have been rephrased in the format of a Self-Assessment questionnaire, with a seven-criterion scoring system, as explained in this document.

In this format, even with limited background knowledge of Smart

Machines, a manager can quickly review existing operations to determine how they measure up to the standards. This in turn can serve as the starting point of a 'gap analysis' to identify management tools or system elements that might usefully be implemented in the organization to help improve overall performance.

How to use the Self-Assessment

On the following pages are a series of questions to identify to what extent your Smart Machines initiative is complete in comparison to the requirements set in standards.

To facilitate answering the questions, there is a space in front of each question to enter a score on a scale of '1' to '5'.

1 Strongly Disagree

2 Disagree

3 Neutral

4 Agree

5 Strongly Agree

Read the question and rate it with the following in front of mind:

'In my belief,
the answer to this question is clearly defined'.

There are two ways in which you can choose to interpret this statement;
1. how aware are you that the answer to the question is clearly defined
2. for more in-depth analysis you can choose to gather

evidence and confirm the answer to the question. This obviously will take more time, most Self-Assessment users opt for the first way to interpret the question and dig deeper later on based on the outcome of the overall Self-Assessment.

A score of '1' would mean that the answer is not clear at all, where a '5' would mean the answer is crystal clear and defined. Leave emtpy when the question is not applicable or you don't want to answer it, you can skip it without affecting your score. Write your score in the space provided.

After you have responded to all the appropriate statements in each section, compute your average score for that section, using the formula provided, and round to the nearest tenth. Then transfer to the corresponding spoke in the Smart Machines Scorecard on the second next page of the Self-Assessment.

Your completed Smart Machines Scorecard will give you a clear presentation of which Smart Machines areas need attention.

Smart Machines Scorecard Example

Example of how the finalized Scorecard can look like:

Smart Machines
Scorecard

Your Scores:

BEGINNING OF THE SELF-ASSESSMENT:

CRITERION #1: RECOGNIZE

INTENT: Be aware of the need for change. Recognize that there is an unfavorable variation, problem or symptom.

In my belief, the answer to this question is clearly defined:

5 Strongly Agree

4 Agree

3 Neutral

2 Disagree

1 Strongly Disagree

1. Can management personnel recognize the monetary benefit of Smart Machines?
<--- Score

2. What should be considered when identifying available resources, constraints, and deadlines?
<--- Score

3. Will new equipment/products be required to

facilitate Smart Machines delivery, for example is new software needed?

<--- Score

4. Will it solve real problems?

<--- Score

5. How much are sponsors, customers, partners, stakeholders involved in Smart Machines? In other words, what are the risks, if Smart Machines does not deliver successfully?

<--- Score

6. Is it clear when you think of the day ahead of you what activities and tasks you need to complete?

<--- Score

7. Think about the people you identified for your Smart Machines project and the project responsibilities you would assign to them. what kind of training do you think they would need to perform these responsibilities effectively?

<--- Score

8. When a Smart Machines manager recognizes a problem, what options are available?

<--- Score

9. Do you know what you need to know about Smart Machines?

<--- Score

10. Does Smart Machines create potential expectations in other areas that need to be recognized and considered?

<--- Score

11. How can auditing be a preventative security measure?
<--- Score

12. What else needs to be measured?
<--- Score

13. How do you identify the kinds of information that you will need?
<--- Score

14. Are controls defined to recognize and contain problems?
<--- Score

15. As a sponsor, customer or management, how important is it to meet goals, objectives?
<--- Score

16. What is the smallest subset of the problem you can usefully solve?
<--- Score

17. Have you identified your Smart Machines key performance indicators?
<--- Score

18. What are the business objectives to be achieved with Smart Machines?
<--- Score

19. What does Smart Machines success mean to the stakeholders?
<--- Score

20. Who else hopes to benefit from it?
<--- Score

21. How do you assess your Smart Machines workforce capability and capacity needs, including skills, competencies, and staffing levels?
<--- Score

22. What are the expected benefits of Smart Machines to the business?
<--- Score

23. Who defines the rules in relation to any given issue?
<--- Score

24. What are your needs in relation to Smart Machines skills, labor, equipment, and markets?
<--- Score

25. What situation(s) led to this Smart Machines Self Assessment?
<--- Score

26. What prevents you from making the changes you know will make you a more effective Smart Machines leader?
<--- Score

27. What would happen if Smart Machines weren't done?
<--- Score

28. What information do users need?
<--- Score

29. What vendors make products that address the Smart Machines needs?
<--- Score

30. How do you take a forward-looking perspective in identifying Smart Machines research related to market response and models?
<--- Score

31. Will Smart Machines deliverables need to be tested and, if so, by whom?
<--- Score

32. What training and capacity building actions are needed to implement proposed reforms?
<--- Score

33. What problems are you facing and how do you consider Smart Machines will circumvent those obstacles?
<--- Score

34. Are there Smart Machines problems defined?
<--- Score

35. What tools and technologies are needed for a custom Smart Machines project?
<--- Score

36. What do you need to start doing?
<--- Score

37. Are there any specific expectations or concerns about the Smart Machines team, Smart Machines itself?
<--- Score

38. How are the Smart Machines's objectives aligned to the organization's overall business strategy?
<--- Score

39. Does your organization need more Smart Machines education?
<--- Score

40. Are there recognized Smart Machines problems?
<--- Score

41. Who had the original idea?
<--- Score

42. How does it fit into your organizational needs and tasks?
<--- Score

43. Will a response program recognize when a crisis occurs and provide some level of response?
<--- Score

44. Consider your own Smart Machines project, what types of organizational problems do you think might be causing or affecting your problem, based on the work done so far?
<--- Score

45. For your Smart Machines project, identify and describe the business environment, is there more than one layer to the business environment?
<--- Score

46. Who needs to know about Smart Machines?
<--- Score

47. How are you going to measure success?
<--- Score

Add up total points for this section:
_____ = Total points for this section

Divided by: _____ (number of statements answered) = _____ Average score for this section

Transfer your score to the Smart Machines Index at the beginning of the Self-Assessment.

CRITERION #2: DEFINE:

INTENT: Formulate the business problem. Define the problem, needs and objectives.

In my belief, the answer to this question is clearly defined:

5 Strongly Agree

4 Agree

3 Neutral

2 Disagree

1 Strongly Disagree

1. How will the Smart Machines team and the organization measure complete success of Smart Machines?
<--- Score

2. How did the Smart Machines manager receive input to the development of a Smart Machines improvement plan and the estimated completion dates/times of each activity?

<--- Score

3. What baselines are required to be defined and managed?
<--- Score

4. Are improvement team members fully trained on Smart Machines?
<--- Score

5. How do you keep key subject matter experts in the loop?
<--- Score

6. Is there a completed, verified, and validated high-level 'as is' (not 'should be' or 'could be') business process map?
<--- Score

7. Is a fully trained team formed, supported, and committed to work on the Smart Machines improvements?
<--- Score

8. Are customers identified and high impact areas defined?
<--- Score

9. What specifically is the problem? Where does it occur? When does it occur? What is its extent?
<--- Score

10. What are the rough order estimates on cost savings/opportunities that Smart Machines brings?
<--- Score

11. Have all basic functions of Smart Machines been defined?
<--- Score

12. Will team members perform Smart Machines work when assigned and in a timely fashion?
<--- Score

13. Are there different segments of customers?
<--- Score

14. If substitutes have been appointed, have they been briefed on the Smart Machines goals and received regular communications as to the progress to date?
<--- Score

15. Is there a completed SIPOC representation, describing the Suppliers, Inputs, Process, Outputs, and Customers?
<--- Score

16. Has a project plan, Gantt chart, or similar been developed/completed?
<--- Score

17. Has a team charter been developed and communicated?
<--- Score

18. Is Smart Machines currently on schedule according to the plan?
<--- Score

19. What key business process output measure(s) does Smart Machines leverage and how?

<--- Score

20. How will variation in the actual durations of each activity be dealt with to ensure that the expected Smart Machines results are met?
<--- Score

21. Has the Smart Machines work been fairly and/ or equitably divided and delegated among team members who are qualified and capable to perform the work? Has everyone contributed?
<--- Score

22. Is it clearly defined in and to your organization what you do?
<--- Score

23. What critical content must be communicated – who, what, when, where, and how?
<--- Score

24. Has anyone else (internal or external to the organization) attempted to solve this problem or a similar one before? If so, what knowledge can be leveraged from these previous efforts?
<--- Score

25. Do you all define Smart Machines in the same way?
<--- Score

26. Are team charters developed?
<--- Score

27. Is the team equipped with available and reliable resources?

<--- Score

28. When was the Smart Machines start date?
<--- Score

29. When is the estimated completion date?
<--- Score

30. Is the team sponsored by a champion or business leader?
<--- Score

31. What constraints exist that might impact the team?
<--- Score

32. What are the record-keeping requirements of Smart Machines activities?
<--- Score

33. Are approval levels defined for contracts and supplements to contracts?
<--- Score

34. What are the dynamics of the communication plan?
<--- Score

35. What are the Roles and Responsibilities for each team member and its leadership? Where is this documented?
<--- Score

36. Have the customer needs been translated into specific, measurable requirements? How?
<--- Score

37. How and when will the baselines be defined?
<--- Score

38. Has the direction changed at all during the course of Smart Machines? If so, when did it change and why?
<--- Score

39. Are roles and responsibilities formally defined?
<--- Score

40. Is the scope of Smart Machines defined?
<--- Score

41. Who are the Smart Machines improvement team members, including Management Leads and Coaches?
<--- Score

42. Are task requirements clearly defined?
<--- Score

43. Do the problem and goal statements meet the SMART criteria (specific, measurable, attainable, relevant, and time-bound)?
<--- Score

44. Is there a critical path to deliver Smart Machines results?
<--- Score

45. How was the 'as is' process map developed, reviewed, verified and validated?
<--- Score

46. Is the team adequately staffed with the desired cross-functionality? If not, what additional resources are available to the team?
<--- Score

47. Have specific policy objectives been defined?
<--- Score

48. Are required metrics defined, what are they?
<--- Score

49. How is the team tracking and documenting its work?
<--- Score

50. Is data collected and displayed to better understand customer(s) critical needs and requirements.
<--- Score

51. Are audit criteria, scope, frequency and methods defined?
<--- Score

52. How often are the team meetings?
<--- Score

53. Are different versions of process maps needed to account for the different types of inputs?
<--- Score

54. Will team members regularly document their Smart Machines work?
<--- Score

55. Are accountability and ownership for Smart

Machines clearly defined?
<--- Score

56. How would you define Smart Machines
leadership?
<--- Score

57. Is the team formed and are team leaders (Coaches
and Management Leads) assigned?
<--- Score

58. Is the improvement team aware of the different
versions of a process: what they think it is vs. what it
actually is vs. what it should be vs. what it could be?
<--- Score

59. How would you define the culture at your
organization, how susceptible is it to Smart Machines
changes?
<--- Score

60. Are business processes mapped?
<--- Score

61. In what way can you redefine the criteria of choice
clients have in your category in your favor?
<--- Score

62. Who defines (or who defined) the rules and roles?
<--- Score

63. Has a high-level 'as is' process map been
completed, verified and validated?
<--- Score

64. Is the Smart Machines scope manageable?

<--- Score

65. Is the current 'as is' process being followed? If not, what are the discrepancies?
<--- Score

66. Is there regularly 100% attendance at the team meetings? If not, have appointed substitutes attended to preserve cross-functionality and full representation?
<--- Score

67. Are customer(s) identified and segmented according to their different needs and requirements?
<--- Score

68. Are there any constraints known that bear on the ability to perform Smart Machines work? How is the team addressing them?
<--- Score

69. What would be the goal or target for a Smart Machines's improvement team?
<--- Score

70. Does the team have regular meetings?
<--- Score

71. How can the value of Smart Machines be defined?
<--- Score

72. Is there a Smart Machines management charter, including business case, problem and goal statements, scope, milestones, roles and responsibilities, communication plan?
<--- Score

73. What are the boundaries of the scope? What is in bounds and what is not? What is the start point? What is the stop point?
<--- Score

74. Has the improvement team collected the 'voice of the customer' (obtained feedback – qualitative and quantitative)?
<--- Score

75. What customer feedback methods were used to solicit their input?
<--- Score

76. Is Smart Machines linked to key business goals and objectives?
<--- Score

77. When are meeting minutes sent out? Who is on the distribution list?
<--- Score

78. Is full participation by members in regularly held team meetings guaranteed?
<--- Score

79. Has/have the customer(s) been identified?
<--- Score

80. Have all of the relationships been defined properly?
<--- Score

81. How does the Smart Machines manager ensure against scope creep?

<--- Score

82. Is Smart Machines required?
<--- Score

83. Has everyone on the team, including the team leaders, been properly trained?
<--- Score

84. What are the compelling business reasons for embarking on Smart Machines?
<--- Score

85. What defines best in class?
<--- Score

86. In what way can you redefine the criteria of choice in your category in your favor?
<--- Score

Add up total points for this section:
_ _ _ _ _ = Total points for this section

Divided by: _ _ _ _ _ _ (number of statements answered) = _ _ _ _ _ _
Average score for this section

Transfer your score to the Smart Machines Index at the beginning of the Self-Assessment.

CRITERION #3: MEASURE:

INTENT: Gather the correct data. Measure the current performance and evolution of the situation.

In my belief, the answer to this question is clearly defined:

5 Strongly Agree

4 Agree

3 Neutral

2 Disagree

1 Strongly Disagree

1. Does your organization systematically track and analyze outcomes related for accountability and quality improvement?
<--- Score

2. How will measures be used to manage and adapt?
<--- Score

3. How to measure variability?

<--- Score

4. What are the key input variables? What are the key process variables? What are the key output variables?
<--- Score

5. What relevant entities could be measured?
<--- Score

6. Is long term and short term variability accounted for?
<--- Score

7. Are the measurements objective?
<--- Score

8. What is measured? Why?
<--- Score

9. What are the types and number of measures to use?
<--- Score

10. What evidence is there and what is measured?
<--- Score

11. How is the value delivered by Smart Machines being measured?
<--- Score

12. How will you measure success?
<--- Score

13. Is it possible to estimate the impact of unanticipated complexity such as wrong or failed assumptions, feedback, etc. on proposed reforms?
<--- Score

14. How frequently do you track measures?
<--- Score

15. Which stakeholder characteristics are analyzed?
<--- Score

16. Is key measure data collection planned
and executed, process variation displayed and
communicated and performance baselined?
<--- Score

17. Among the Smart Machines product and service
cost to be estimated, which is considered hardest to
estimate?
<--- Score

18. Do you aggressively reward and promote the
people who have the biggest impact on creating
excellent Smart Machines services/products?
<--- Score

19. What is an unallowable cost?
<--- Score

20. Is the solution cost-effective?
<--- Score

21. How do you measure lifecycle phases?
<--- Score

22. How will your organization measure success?
<--- Score

23. Are key measures identified and agreed upon?
<--- Score

24. Does Smart Machines systematically track and analyze outcomes for accountability and quality improvement?
<--- Score

25. Which measures and indicators matter?
<--- Score

26. Have you found any 'ground fruit' or 'low-hanging fruit' for immediate remedies to the gap in performance?
<--- Score

27. What particular quality tools did the team find helpful in establishing measurements?
<--- Score

28. How is progress measured?
<--- Score

29. What measurements are possible, practicable and meaningful?
<--- Score

30. How do you stay flexible and focused to recognize larger Smart Machines results?
<--- Score

31. Are process variation components displayed/communicated using suitable charts, graphs, plots?
<--- Score

32. How do your measurements capture actionable Smart Machines information for use in exceeding your customers expectations and securing your customers

engagement?
<--- Score

33. What charts has the team used to display the components of variation in the process?
<--- Score

34. Is data collection planned and executed?
<--- Score

35. How frequently do you track Smart Machines measures?
<--- Score

36. Does the Smart Machines task fit the client's priorities?
<--- Score

37. Are high impact defects defined and identified in the business process?
<--- Score

38. Is data collected on key measures that were identified?
<--- Score

39. Why do you expend time and effort to implement measurement, for whom?
<--- Score

40. What data was collected (past, present, future/ongoing)?
<--- Score

41. Are the units of measure consistent?
<--- Score

42. Are missed Smart Machines opportunities costing your organization money?
<--- Score

43. Can you measure the return on analysis?
<--- Score

44. What has the team done to assure the stability and accuracy of the measurement process?
<--- Score

45. How do you control the overall costs of your work processes?
<--- Score

46. How can you measure Smart Machines in a systematic way?
<--- Score

47. How do you aggregate measures across priorities?
<--- Score

48. How do you measure success?
<--- Score

49. How do you identify and analyze stakeholders and their interests?
<--- Score

50. What are the costs of reform?
<--- Score

51. Have changes been properly/adequately analyzed for effect?
<--- Score

52. Does Smart Machines analysis isolate the fundamental causes of problems?
<--- Score

53. Who participated in the data collection for measurements?
<--- Score

54. What is the total cost related to deploying Smart Machines, including any consulting or professional services?
<--- Score

55. How are measurements made?
<--- Score

56. What potential environmental factors impact the Smart Machines effort?
<--- Score

57. Are losses documented, analyzed, and remedial processes developed to prevent future losses?
<--- Score

58. Can you do Smart Machines without complex (expensive) analysis?
<--- Score

59. What do you measure and why?
<--- Score

60. How are you going to measure success?
<--- Score

61. Is a solid data collection plan established that

includes measurement systems analysis?
<--- Score

62. What are your key Smart Machines organizational performance measures, including key short and longer-term financial measures?
<--- Score

63. Where is it measured?
<--- Score

64. Will Smart Machines have an impact on current business continuity, disaster recovery processes and/ or infrastructure?
<--- Score

65. How will effects be measured?
<--- Score

66. Who should receive measurement reports?
<--- Score

67. Does Smart Machines analysis show the relationships among important Smart Machines factors?
<--- Score

68. How will success or failure be measured?
<--- Score

69. How can you measure the performance?
<--- Score

70. Are there any easy-to-implement alternatives to Smart Machines? Sometimes other solutions are available that do not require the cost implications of a

full-blown project?
<--- Score

71. Is Process Variation Displayed/Communicated?
<--- Score

72. Do you effectively measure and reward individual and team performance?
<--- Score

73. What are your key Smart Machines indicators that you will measure, analyze and track?
<--- Score

74. How is performance measured?
<--- Score

75. Is there a Performance Baseline?
<--- Score

76. What are the uncertainties surrounding estimates of impact?
<--- Score

77. Why do the measurements/indicators matter?
<--- Score

78. Was a data collection plan established?
<--- Score

79. What measurements are being captured?
<--- Score

80. Are there measurements based on task performance?
<--- Score

81. How do you do risk analysis of rare, cascading, catastrophic events?
<--- Score

82. What are your customers expectations and measures?
<--- Score

83. How do you focus on what is right -not who is right?
<--- Score

84. How large is the gap between current performance and the customer-specified (goal) performance?
<--- Score

85. Are you taking your company in the direction of better and revenue or cheaper and cost?
<--- Score

86. What methods are feasible and acceptable to estimate the impact of reforms?
<--- Score

87. How do you know that any Smart Machines analysis is complete and comprehensive?
<--- Score

88. How will you measure your Smart Machines effectiveness?
<--- Score

89. What are the agreed upon definitions of the high impact areas, defect(s), unit(s), and opportunities that

will figure into the process capability metrics?
<--- Score

90. What key measures identified indicate the performance of the business process?
<--- Score

91. Have all non-recommended alternatives been analyzed in sufficient detail?
<--- Score

92. Do staff have the necessary skills to collect, analyze, and report data?
<--- Score

93. What is the right balance of time and resources between investigation, analysis, and discussion and dissemination?
<--- Score

94. Have the concerns of stakeholders to help identify and define potential barriers been obtained and analyzed?
<--- Score

95. The approach of traditional Smart Machines works for detail complexity but is focused on a systematic approach rather than an understanding of the nature of systems themselves, what approach will permit your organization to deal with the kind of unpredictable emergent behaviors that dynamic complexity can introduce?
<--- Score

96. Have the types of risks that may impact Smart Machines been identified and analyzed?

<--- Score

Add up total points for this section:

_____ = Total points for this section

Divided by: _____ (number of
statements answered) = _____
Average score for this section

Transfer your score to the Smart
Machines Index at the beginning of the
Self-Assessment.

CRITERION #4: ANALYZE:

INTENT: Analyze causes, assumptions and hypotheses.

In my belief, the answer to this question is clearly defined:

5 Strongly Agree

4 Agree

3 Neutral

2 Disagree

1 Strongly Disagree

1. When conducting a business process reengineering study, what do you look for when trying to identify business processes to change?
<--- Score

2. What does the data say about the performance of the business process?
<--- Score

3. Have the problem and goal statements been

updated to reflect the additional knowledge gained from the analyze phase?
<--- Score

4. Were Pareto charts (or similar) used to portray the 'heavy hitters' (or key sources of variation)?
<--- Score

5. Identify an operational issue in your organization. for example, could a particular task be done more quickly or more efficiently by Smart Machines?
<--- Score

6. An organizationally feasible system request is one that considers the mission, goals and objectives of the organization. Key questions are: is the Smart Machines solution request practical and will it solve a problem or take advantage of an opportunity to achieve company goals?
<--- Score

7. Do your leaders quickly bounce back from setbacks?
<--- Score

8. Is the suppliers process defined and controlled?
<--- Score

9. What were the crucial 'moments of truth' on the process map?
<--- Score

10. What successful thing are you doing today that may be blinding you to new growth opportunities?
<--- Score

11. Where is the data coming from to measure compliance?
<--- Score

12. How do you use Smart Machines data and information to support organizational decision making and innovation?
<--- Score

13. What did the team gain from developing a sub-process map?
<--- Score

14. What were the financial benefits resulting from any 'ground fruit or low-hanging fruit' (quick fixes)?
<--- Score

15. How was the detailed process map generated, verified, and validated?
<--- Score

16. How do you identify specific Smart Machines investment opportunities and emerging trends?
<--- Score

17. What process should you select for improvement?
<--- Score

18. Did any value-added analysis or 'lean thinking' take place to identify some of the gaps shown on the 'as is' process map?
<--- Score

19. Record-keeping requirements flow from the records needed as inputs, outputs, controls and for transformation of a Smart Machines process. Are

the records needed as inputs to the Smart Machines process available?
<--- Score

20. How often will data be collected for measures?
<--- Score

21. How is the way you as the leader think and process information affecting your organizational culture?
<--- Score

22. Were any designed experiments used to generate additional insight into the data analysis?
<--- Score

23. What other organizational variables, such as reward systems or communication systems, affect the performance of this Smart Machines process?
<--- Score

24. What are the revised rough estimates of the financial savings/opportunity for Smart Machines improvements?
<--- Score

25. Is the Smart Machines process severely broken such that a re-design is necessary?
<--- Score

26. Was a detailed process map created to amplify critical steps of the 'as is' business process?
<--- Score

27. Can you add value to the current Smart Machines decision-making process (largely qualitative) by incorporating uncertainty modeling (more

quantitative)?
<--- Score

28. What are the best opportunities for value improvement?
<--- Score

29. A compounding model resolution with available relevant data can often provide insight towards a solution methodology; which Smart Machines models, tools and techniques are necessary?
<--- Score

30. Was a cause-and-effect diagram used to explore the different types of causes (or sources of variation)?
<--- Score

31. How do you implement and manage your work processes to ensure that they meet design requirements?
<--- Score

32. Think about some of the processes you undertake within your organization, which do you own?
<--- Score

33. What is the cost of poor quality as supported by the team's analysis?
<--- Score

34. What are the disruptive Smart Machines technologies that enable your organization to radically change your business processes?
<--- Score

35. What are your current levels and trends in key

Smart Machines measures or indicators of product and process performance that are important to and directly serve your customers?
<--- Score

36. What are your Smart Machines processes?
<--- Score

37. Were there any improvement opportunities identified from the process analysis?
<--- Score

38. Think about the functions involved in your Smart Machines project, what processes flow from these functions?
<--- Score

39. How does the organization define, manage, and improve its Smart Machines processes?
<--- Score

40. What quality tools were used to get through the analyze phase?
<--- Score

41. Do your employees have the opportunity to do what they do best everyday?
<--- Score

42. Do several people in different organizational units assist with the Smart Machines process?
<--- Score

43. Have any additional benefits been identified that will result from closing all or most of the gaps?
<--- Score

44. What tools were used to generate the list of possible causes?
<--- Score

45. Is the gap/opportunity displayed and communicated in financial terms?
<--- Score

46. How do mission and objectives affect the Smart Machines processes of your organization?
<--- Score

47. How do you promote understanding that opportunity for improvement is not criticism of the status quo, or the people who created the status quo?
<--- Score

48. How do your work systems and key work processes relate to and capitalize on your core competencies?
<--- Score

49. Is Data and process analysis, root cause analysis and quantifying the gap/opportunity in place?
<--- Score

50. What tools were used to narrow the list of possible causes?
<--- Score

51. What conclusions were drawn from the team's data collection and analysis? How did the team reach these conclusions?
<--- Score

52. Do you, as a leader, bounce back quickly from setbacks?
<--- Score

53. Is the performance gap determined?
<--- Score

54. What are your key performance measures or indicators and in-process measures for the control and improvement of your Smart Machines processes?
<--- Score

55. What are your best practices for minimizing Smart Machines project risk, while demonstrating incremental value and quick wins throughout the Smart Machines project lifecycle?
<--- Score

56. What are your current levels and trends in key measures or indicators of Smart Machines product and process performance that are important to and directly serve your customers? How do these results compare with the performance of your competitors and other organizations with similar offerings?
<--- Score

57. What other jobs or tasks affect the performance of the steps in the Smart Machines process?
<--- Score

58. Did any additional data need to be collected?
<--- Score

59. What controls do you have in place to protect data?
<--- Score

60. Are gaps between current performance and the goal performance identified?
<--- Score

61. How do you measure the operational performance of your key work systems and processes, including productivity, cycle time, and other appropriate measures of process effectiveness, efficiency, and innovation?
<--- Score

Add up total points for this section:
_____ = Total points for this section

Divided by: _____ (number of statements answered) = _____ Average score for this section

Transfer your score to the Smart Machines Index at the beginning of the Self-Assessment.

CRITERION #5: IMPROVE:

INTENT: Develop a practical solution. Innovate, establish and test the solution and to measure the results.

In my belief, the answer to this question is clearly defined:

5 Strongly Agree

4 Agree

3 Neutral

2 Disagree

1 Strongly Disagree

1. What tools do you use once you have decided on a Smart Machines strategy and more importantly how do you choose?
<--- Score

2. How did the team generate the list of possible solutions?
<--- Score

3. How do you measure progress and evaluate training effectiveness?
<--- Score

4. How does the solution remove the key sources of issues discovered in the analyze phase?
<--- Score

5. Why improve in the first place?
<--- Score

6. Explorations of the frontiers of Smart Machines will help you build influence, improve Smart Machines, optimize decision making, and sustain change, what is your approach?
<--- Score

7. What tools were most useful during the improve phase?
<--- Score

8. What does the 'should be' process map/design look like?
<--- Score

9. Do you combine technical expertise with business knowledge and Smart Machines Key topics include lifecycles, development approaches, requirements and how to make a business case?
<--- Score

10. How do you link measurement and risk?
<--- Score

11. How do you keep improving Smart Machines?
<--- Score

12. Who controls key decisions that will be made?
<--- Score

13. Is there a cost/benefit analysis of optimal solution(s)?
<--- Score

14. How will the organization know that the solution worked?
<--- Score

15. How can you improve performance?
<--- Score

16. For decision problems, how do you develop a decision statement?
<--- Score

17. How does the team improve its work?
<--- Score

18. Risk factors: what are the characteristics of Smart Machines that make it risky?
<--- Score

19. Is a contingency plan established?
<--- Score

20. To what extent does management recognize Smart Machines as a tool to increase the results?
<--- Score

21. How will you know that a change is an improvement?
<--- Score

22. Who will be using the results of the measurement activities?
<--- Score

23. How do you improve your likelihood of success ?
<--- Score

24. How do you measure improved Smart Machines service perception, and satisfaction?
<--- Score

25. Does the goal represent a desired result that can be measured?
<--- Score

26. What can you do to improve?
<--- Score

27. Who will be responsible for documenting the Smart Machines requirements in detail?
<--- Score

28. How will the team or the process owner(s) monitor the implementation plan to see that it is working as intended?
<--- Score

29. What are your current levels and trends in key measures or indicators of workforce and leader development?
<--- Score

30. Is pilot data collected and analyzed?
<--- Score

31. What tools were used to evaluate the potential solutions?
<--- Score

32. What communications are necessary to support the implementation of the solution?
<--- Score

33. What needs improvement? Why?
<--- Score

34. How do the Smart Machines results compare with the performance of your competitors and other organizations with similar offerings?
<--- Score

35. Who are the people involved in developing and implementing Smart Machines?
<--- Score

36. At what point will vulnerability assessments be performed once Smart Machines is put into production (e.g., ongoing Risk Management after implementation)?
<--- Score

37. Do those selected for the Smart Machines team have a good general understanding of what Smart Machines is all about?
<--- Score

38. Are the best solutions selected?
<--- Score

39. What to do with the results or outcomes of measurements?

<--- Score

40. Is the solution technically practical?
<--- Score

41. What is Smart Machines's impact on utilizing the best solution(s)?
<--- Score

42. Can the solution be designed and implemented within an acceptable time period?
<--- Score

43. Do you cover the five essential competencies: Communication, Collaboration,Innovation, Adaptability, and Leadership that improve an organization's ability to leverage the new Smart Machines in a volatile global economy?
<--- Score

44. Are there any constraints (technical, political, cultural, or otherwise) that would inhibit certain solutions?
<--- Score

45. Are new and improved process ('should be') maps developed?
<--- Score

46. What are the implications of the one critical Smart Machines decision 10 minutes, 10 months, and 10 years from now?
<--- Score

47. If you could go back in time five years, what decision would you make differently? What is your

best guess as to what decision you're making today you might regret five years from now?
<--- Score

48. Are you assessing Smart Machines and risk?
<--- Score

49. For estimation problems, how do you develop an estimation statement?
<--- Score

50. What improvements have been achieved?
<--- Score

51. What lessons, if any, from a pilot were incorporated into the design of the full-scale solution?
<--- Score

52. How do you improve Smart Machines service perception, and satisfaction?
<--- Score

53. What went well, what should change, what can improve?
<--- Score

54. Is the implementation plan designed?
<--- Score

55. Are improved process ('should be') maps modified based on pilot data and analysis?
<--- Score

56. What is the team's contingency plan for potential problems occurring in implementation?
<--- Score

57. What attendant changes will need to be made to ensure that the solution is successful?
<--- Score

58. How can you improve Smart Machines?
<--- Score

59. What were the underlying assumptions on the cost-benefit analysis?
<--- Score

60. Are possible solutions generated and tested?
<--- Score

61. Is there a small-scale pilot for proposed improvement(s)? What conclusions were drawn from the outcomes of a pilot?
<--- Score

62. What resources are required for the improvement efforts?
<--- Score

63. How will you know when its improved?
<--- Score

64. Risk events: what are the things that could go wrong?
<--- Score

65. How do you manage and improve your Smart Machines work systems to deliver customer value and achieve organizational success and sustainability?
<--- Score

66. Were any criteria developed to assist the team in testing and evaluating potential solutions?
<--- Score

67. How can skill-level changes improve Smart Machines?
<--- Score

68. In the past few months, what is the smallest change you have made that has had the biggest positive result? What was it about that small change that produced the large return?
<--- Score

69. How do you improve productivity?
<--- Score

70. Is supporting Smart Machines documentation required?
<--- Score

71. Is the measure of success for Smart Machines understandable to a variety of people?
<--- Score

72. What is the Smart Machines's sustainability risk?
<--- Score

73. What tools were used to tap into the creativity and encourage 'outside the box' thinking?
<--- Score

74. Who will be responsible for making the decisions to include or exclude requested changes once Smart Machines is underway?
<--- Score

75. Describe the design of the pilot and what tests were conducted, if any?
<--- Score

76. How do you go about comparing Smart Machines approaches/solutions?
<--- Score

77. What is the implementation plan?
<--- Score

78. Was a pilot designed for the proposed solution(s)?
<--- Score

79. What is the magnitude of the improvements?
<--- Score

80. Is there a high likelihood that any recommendations will achieve their intended results?
<--- Score

81. What do you want to improve?
<--- Score

82. How significant is the improvement in the eyes of the end user?
<--- Score

83. Is a solution implementation plan established, including schedule/work breakdown structure, resources, risk management plan, cost/budget, and control plan?
<--- Score

84. Is the optimal solution selected based on testing

and analysis?
<--- Score

85. How will you know that you have improved?
<--- Score

86. How do you measure risk?
<--- Score

87. What is the risk?
<--- Score

88. What should a proof of concept or pilot accomplish?
<--- Score

89. What actually has to improve and by how much?
<--- Score

90. Who controls the risk?
<--- Score

91. How will you measure the results?
<--- Score

92. What error proofing will be done to address some of the discrepancies observed in the 'as is' process?
<--- Score

93. How do you decide how much to remunerate an employee?
<--- Score

Add up total points for this section:
_ _ _ _ _ = Total points for this section

Divided by: _____ (number of
statements answered) = _____
Average score for this section

Transfer your score to the Smart
Machines Index at the beginning of the
Self-Assessment.

CRITERION #6: CONTROL:

INTENT: Implement the practical solution. Maintain the performance and correct possible complications.

In my belief, the answer to this question is clearly defined:

5 Strongly Agree

4 Agree

3 Neutral

2 Disagree

1 Strongly Disagree

1. What are the known security controls?
<--- Score

2. How will input, process, and output variables be checked to detect for sub-optimal conditions?
<--- Score

3. Implementation Planning- is a pilot needed to test the changes before a full roll out occurs?

<--- Score

4. What are the key elements of your Smart Machines performance improvement system, including your evaluation, organizational learning, and innovation processes?
<--- Score

5. Is there a standardized process?
<--- Score

6. What key inputs and outputs are being measured on an ongoing basis?
<--- Score

7. How will the process owner verify improvement in present and future sigma levels, process capabilities?
<--- Score

8. What do you measure to verify effectiveness gains?
<--- Score

9. Is there a recommended audit plan for routine surveillance inspections of Smart Machines's gains?
<--- Score

10. Are new process steps, standards, and documentation ingrained into normal operations?
<--- Score

11. Are documented procedures clear and easy to follow for the operators?
<--- Score

12. How likely is the current Smart Machines plan to come in on schedule or on budget?

<--- Score

13. You may have created your quality measures at a time when you lacked resources, technology wasn't up to the required standard, or low service levels were the industry norm. Have those circumstances changed?
<--- Score

14. Are the planned controls in place?
<--- Score

15. Will existing staff require re-training, for example, to learn new business processes?
<--- Score

16. How do you encourage people to take control and responsibility?
<--- Score

17. How will the process owner and team be able to hold the gains?
<--- Score

18. Who will be in control?
<--- Score

19. What are your results for key measures or indicators of the accomplishment of your Smart Machines strategy and action plans, including building and strengthening core competencies?
<--- Score

20. Do you monitor the effectiveness of your Smart Machines activities?
<--- Score

21. What other areas of the organization might benefit from the Smart Machines team's improvements, knowledge, and learning?
<--- Score

22. Are the planned controls working?
<--- Score

23. How do your controls stack up?
<--- Score

24. Does a troubleshooting guide exist or is it needed?
<--- Score

25. What do you stand for--and what are you against?
<--- Score

26. What should the next improvement project be that is related to Smart Machines?
<--- Score

27. Is a response plan established and deployed?
<--- Score

28. Does the Smart Machines performance meet the customer's requirements?
<--- Score

29. Are there documented procedures?
<--- Score

30. How will new or emerging customer needs/requirements be checked/communicated to orient the process toward meeting the new specifications and continually reducing variation?

<--- Score

31. What other systems, operations, processes, and infrastructures (hiring practices, staffing, training, incentives/rewards, metrics/dashboards/scorecards, etc.) need updates, additions, changes, or deletions in order to facilitate knowledge transfer and improvements?
<--- Score

32. Who is the Smart Machines process owner?
<--- Score

33. What quality tools were useful in the control phase?
<--- Score

34. How will the day-to-day responsibilities for monitoring and continual improvement be transferred from the improvement team to the process owner?
<--- Score

35. Does the response plan contain a definite closed loop continual improvement scheme (e.g., plan-do-check-act)?
<--- Score

36. What is the best design framework for Smart Machines organization now that, in a post industrial-age if the top-down, command and control model is no longer relevant?
<--- Score

37. What is the recommended frequency of auditing?
<--- Score

38. Are controls in place and consistently applied?
<--- Score

39. Will any special training be provided for results interpretation?
<--- Score

40. Has the improved process and its steps been standardized?
<--- Score

41. Who controls critical resources?
<--- Score

42. How do you select, collect, align, and integrate Smart Machines data and information for tracking daily operations and overall organizational performance, including progress relative to strategic objectives and action plans?
<--- Score

43. How might the organization capture best practices and lessons learned so as to leverage improvements across the business?
<--- Score

44. What can you control?
<--- Score

45. Do the decisions you make today help people and the planet tomorrow?
<--- Score

46. Is a response plan in place for when the input, process, or output measures indicate an 'out-of-

control' condition?
<--- Score

47. Are operating procedures consistent?
<--- Score

48. What is the control/monitoring plan?
<--- Score

49. Does Smart Machines appropriately measure and monitor risk?
<--- Score

50. What is your theory of human motivation, and how does your compensation plan fit with that view?
<--- Score

51. Is there a transfer of ownership and knowledge to process owner and process team tasked with the responsibilities.
<--- Score

52. Against what alternative is success being measured?
<--- Score

53. Are you measuring, monitoring and predicting Smart Machines activities to optimize operations and profitability, and enhancing outcomes?
<--- Score

54. Does job training on the documented procedures need to be part of the process team's education and training?
<--- Score

55. What should you measure to verify efficiency gains?
<--- Score

56. How can you best use all of your knowledge repositories to enhance learning and sharing?
<--- Score

57. Do the Smart Machines decisions you make today help people and the planet tomorrow?
<--- Score

58. Who has control over resources?
<--- Score

59. What are the critical parameters to watch?
<--- Score

60. How will report readings be checked to effectively monitor performance?
<--- Score

61. Who sets the Smart Machines standards?
<--- Score

62. Where do ideas that reach policy makers and planners as proposals for Smart Machines strengthening and reform actually originate?
<--- Score

63. Is there a documented and implemented monitoring plan?
<--- Score

64. How is change control managed?
<--- Score

65. Is knowledge gained on process shared and institutionalized?
<--- Score

66. In the case of a Smart Machines project, the criteria for the audit derive from implementation objectives. an audit of a Smart Machines project involves assessing whether the recommendations outlined for implementation have been met. Can you track that any Smart Machines project is implemented as planned, and is it working?
<--- Score

67. Is there a control plan in place for sustaining improvements (short and long-term)?
<--- Score

68. Are suggested corrective/restorative actions indicated on the response plan for known causes to problems that might surface?
<--- Score

69. Do you monitor the Smart Machines decisions made and fine tune them as they evolve?
<--- Score

70. How do you establish and deploy modified action plans if circumstances require a shift in plans and rapid execution of new plans?
<--- Score

71. Is there a Smart Machines Communication plan covering who needs to get what information when?
<--- Score

72. How do controls support value?
<--- Score

73. Is reporting being used or needed?
<--- Score

74. What are you attempting to measure/monitor?
<--- Score

75. Are pertinent alerts monitored, analyzed and distributed to appropriate personnel?
<--- Score

76. Have new or revised work instructions resulted?
<--- Score

77. Is there documentation that will support the successful operation of the improvement?
<--- Score

78. Is new knowledge gained imbedded in the response plan?
<--- Score

Add up total points for this section:
_ _ _ _ _ = Total points for this section

Divided by: _ _ _ _ _ _ (number of statements answered) = _ _ _ _ _ _
Average score for this section

Transfer your score to the Smart Machines Index at the beginning of the Self-Assessment.

CRITERION #7: SUSTAIN:

INTENT: Retain the benefits.

In my belief, the answer to this question is clearly defined:

5 Strongly Agree

4 Agree

3 Neutral

2 Disagree

1 Strongly Disagree

1. What are the potential basics of Smart Machines fraud?
<--- Score

2. What one word do you want to own in the minds of your customers, employees, and partners?
<--- Score

3. How do you keep records, of what?
<--- Score

4. What counts that you are not counting?
<--- Score

5. Who do you want your customers to become?
<--- Score

6. What are specific Smart Machines rules to follow?
<--- Score

7. How will you know that the Smart Machines project has been successful?
<--- Score

8. Why not do Smart Machines?
<--- Score

9. What sources do you use to gather information for a Smart Machines study?
<--- Score

10. When information truly is ubiquitous, when reach and connectivity are completely global, when computing resources are infinite, and when a whole new set of impossibilities are not only possible, but happening, what will that do to your business?
<--- Score

11. Is there any reason to believe the opposite of my current belief?
<--- Score

12. How do you go about securing Smart Machines?
<--- Score

13. How do customers see your organization?
<--- Score

14. What are internal and external Smart Machines relations?
<--- Score

15. How do you lead with Smart Machines in mind?
<--- Score

16. Who will determine interim and final deadlines?
<--- Score

17. Who are four people whose careers you have enhanced?
<--- Score

18. Do you have an implicit bias for capital investments over people investments?
<--- Score

19. Which Smart Machines goals are the most important?
<--- Score

20. What current systems have to be understood and/or changed?
<--- Score

21. Is Smart Machines realistic, or are you setting yourself up for failure?
<--- Score

22. How much contingency will be available in the budget?
<--- Score

23. Why is Smart Machines important for you now?

<--- Score

24. If you had to rebuild your organization without any traditional competitive advantages (i.e., no killer a technology, promising research, innovative product/ service delivery model, etc.), how would your people have to approach their work and collaborate together in order to create the necessary conditions for success?
<--- Score

25. What role does communication play in the success or failure of a Smart Machines project?
<--- Score

26. If you were responsible for initiating and implementing major changes in your organization, what steps might you take to ensure acceptance of those changes?
<--- Score

27. Have new benefits been realized?
<--- Score

28. If you do not follow, then how to lead?
<--- Score

29. Are the assumptions believable and achievable?
<--- Score

30. Who will be responsible for deciding whether Smart Machines goes ahead or not after the initial investigations?
<--- Score

31. Why should people listen to you?

<--- Score

32. What is your competitive advantage?
<--- Score

33. Would you rather sell to knowledgeable and informed customers or to uninformed customers?
<--- Score

34. What would you recommend your friend do if he/she were facing this dilemma?
<--- Score

35. What is a feasible sequencing of reform initiatives over time?
<--- Score

36. Who is on the team?
<--- Score

37. Why do and why don't your customers like your organization?
<--- Score

38. How do you stay inspired?
<--- Score

39. How do you create buy-in?
<--- Score

40. How do you ensure that implementations of Smart Machines products are done in a way that ensures safety?
<--- Score

41. Operational - will it work?

<--- Score

42. Who have you, as a company, historically been when you've been at your best?
<--- Score

43. What are the success criteria that will indicate that Smart Machines objectives have been met and the benefits delivered?
<--- Score

44. How do you determine the key elements that affect Smart Machines workforce satisfaction, how are these elements determined for different workforce groups and segments?
<--- Score

45. Instead of going to current contacts for new ideas, what if you reconnected with dormant contacts-- the people you used to know? If you were going reactivate a dormant tie, who would it be?
<--- Score

46. What are the challenges?
<--- Score

47. Do you know what you are doing? And who do you call if you don't?
<--- Score

48. Are you using a design thinking approach and integrating Innovation, Smart Machines Experience, and Brand Value?
<--- Score

49. What are the usability implications of Smart

Machines actions?
<--- Score

50. What new services of functionality will be implemented next with Smart Machines ?
<--- Score

51. How do you cross-sell and up-sell your Smart Machines success?
<--- Score

52. Are you / should you be revolutionary or evolutionary?
<--- Score

53. How do you make it meaningful in connecting Smart Machines with what users do day-to-day?
<--- Score

54. What are the long-term Smart Machines goals?
<--- Score

55. What happens when a new employee joins the organization?
<--- Score

56. Is maximizing Smart Machines protection the same as minimizing Smart Machines loss?
<--- Score

57. Do you see more potential in people than they do in themselves?
<--- Score

58. If you had to leave your organization for a year and the only communication you could have with

employees/colleagues was a single paragraph, what would you write?
<--- Score

59. What may be the consequences for the performance of an organization if all stakeholders are not consulted regarding Smart Machines?
<--- Score

60. Is your strategy driving your strategy? Or is the way in which you allocate resources driving your strategy?
<--- Score

61. What do smart machines have to do with your business process management initiatives?
<--- Score

62. How can you negotiate Smart Machines successfully with a stubborn boss, an irate client, or a deceitful coworker?
<--- Score

63. What is something you believe that nearly no one agrees with you on?
<--- Score

64. What is effective Smart Machines?
<--- Score

65. Ask yourself: how would you do this work if you only had one staff member to do it?
<--- Score

66. How will you insure seamless interoperability of Smart Machines moving forward?

<--- Score

67. How do you keep the momentum going?
<--- Score

68. If your customer were your grandmother, would you tell her to buy what you're selling?
<--- Score

69. Were lessons learned captured and communicated?
<--- Score

70. Are new benefits received and understood?
<--- Score

71. How will you ensure you get what you expected?
<--- Score

72. Who do we want your customers to become?
<--- Score

73. What business benefits will Smart Machines goals deliver if achieved?
<--- Score

74. What is the estimated value of the project?
<--- Score

75. What stupid rule would you most like to kill?
<--- Score

76. In the past year, what have you done (or could you have done) to increase the accurate perception of your company/brand as ethical and honest?
<--- Score

77. What kind of crime could a potential new hire have committed that would not only not disqualify him/her from being hired by your organization, but would actually indicate that he/she might be a particularly good fit?
<--- Score

78. What are the top 3 things at the forefront of your Smart Machines agendas for the next 3 years?
<--- Score

79. What trouble can you get into?
<--- Score

80. What should you stop doing?
<--- Score

81. Are you paying enough attention to the partners your company depends on to succeed?
<--- Score

82. What is your Smart Machines strategy?
<--- Score

83. What happens at your organization when people fail?
<--- Score

84. What will drive Smart Machines change?
<--- Score

85. How important is Smart Machines to the user organizations mission?
<--- Score

86. Are you relevant? Will you be relevant five years from now? Ten?
<--- Score

87. What is your formula for success in Smart Machines ?
<--- Score

88. Do you have enough freaky customers in your portfolio pushing you to the limit day in and day out?
<--- Score

89. Are you satisfied with your current role? If not, what is missing from it?
<--- Score

90. At what moment would you think; Will I get fired?
<--- Score

91. Who is responsible for errors?
<--- Score

92. What management system can you use to leverage the Smart Machines experience, ideas, and concerns of the people closest to the work to be done?
<--- Score

93. What do we do when new problems arise?
<--- Score

94. What are the short and long-term Smart Machines goals?
<--- Score

95. To whom do you add value?

<--- Score

96. What is your BATNA (best alternative to a negotiated agreement)?
<--- Score

97. What are you trying to prove to yourself, and how might it be hijacking your life and business success?
<--- Score

98. How do you listen to customers to obtain actionable information?
<--- Score

99. Are the criteria for selecting recommendations stated?
<--- Score

100. How can you become the company that would put you out of business?
<--- Score

101. Whose voice (department, ethnic group, women, older workers, etc) might you have missed hearing from in your company, and how might you amplify this voice to create positive momentum for your business?
<--- Score

102. What information is critical to your organization that your executives are ignoring?
<--- Score

103. How do you engage the workforce, in addition to satisfying them?
<--- Score

104. What does your signature ensure?
<--- Score

105. Who is responsible for ensuring appropriate resources (time, people and money) are allocated to Smart Machines?
<--- Score

106. In a project to restructure Smart Machines outcomes, which stakeholders would you involve?
<--- Score

107. What is the source of the strategies for Smart Machines strengthening and reform?
<--- Score

108. Why is it important to have senior management support for a Smart Machines project?
<--- Score

109. Will it be accepted by users?
<--- Score

110. Political -is anyone trying to undermine this project?
<--- Score

111. How do you proactively clarify deliverables and Smart Machines quality expectations?
<--- Score

112. Are there any disadvantages to implementing Smart Machines? There might be some that are less obvious?
<--- Score

113. What knowledge, skills and characteristics mark a good Smart Machines project manager?
<--- Score

114. What are the business goals Smart Machines is aiming to achieve?
<--- Score

115. How do you maintain Smart Machines's Integrity?
<--- Score

116. Who will provide the final approval of Smart Machines deliverables?
<--- Score

117. Is it economical; do you have the time and money?
<--- Score

118. How do you foster the skills, knowledge, talents, attributes, and characteristics you want to have?
<--- Score

119. How long will it take to change?
<--- Score

120. What is the funding source for this project?
<--- Score

121. If there were zero limitations, what would you do differently?
<--- Score

122. Who, on the executive team or the board, has spoken to a customer recently?

<--- Score

123. Whom among your colleagues do you trust, and for what?
<--- Score

124. What are your most important goals for the strategic Smart Machines objectives?
<--- Score

125. Who uses your product in ways you never expected?
<--- Score

126. How do you provide a safe environment -physically and emotionally?
<--- Score

127. How does Smart Machines integrate with other business initiatives?
<--- Score

128. Do you have the right capabilities and capacities?
<--- Score

129. What is the kind of project structure that would be appropriate for your Smart Machines project, should it be formal and complex, or can it be less formal and relatively simple?
<--- Score

130. How much does Smart Machines help?
<--- Score

131. Which functions and people interact with the supplier and or customer?

<--- Score

132. How do you assess the Smart Machines pitfalls that are inherent in implementing it?
<--- Score

133. Are assumptions made in Smart Machines stated explicitly?
<--- Score

134. Can you maintain your growth without detracting from the factors that have contributed to your success?
<--- Score

135. What are you challenging?
<--- Score

136. What is the craziest thing you can do?
<--- Score

137. What are the barriers to increased Smart Machines production?
<--- Score

138. Do you have the right people on the bus?
<--- Score

139. Do you think you know, or do you know you know ?
<--- Score

140. Think of your Smart Machines project, what are the main functions?
<--- Score

141. What are strategies for increasing support and reducing opposition?
<--- Score

142. How can you incorporate support to ensure safe and effective use of Smart Machines into the services that you provide?
<--- Score

143. How do you accomplish your long range Smart Machines goals?
<--- Score

144. In retrospect, of the projects that you pulled the plug on, what percent do you wish had been allowed to keep going, and what percent do you wish had ended earlier?
<--- Score

145. How do you foster innovation?
<--- Score

146. How do you manage Smart Machines Knowledge Management (KM)?
<--- Score

147. Is a Smart Machines team work effort in place?
<--- Score

148. What happens if you do not have enough funding?
<--- Score

149. What potential megatrends could make your business model obsolete?
<--- Score

150. Are you changing as fast as the world around you?
<--- Score

151. How likely is it that a customer would recommend your company to a friend or colleague?
<--- Score

152. Who is responsible for Smart Machines?
<--- Score

153. How do senior leaders actions reflect a commitment to the organizations Smart Machines values?
<--- Score

154. Did your employees make progress today?
<--- Score

155. How do you know if you are successful?
<--- Score

156. Are you failing differently each time?
<--- Score

157. What is it like to work for you?
<--- Score

158. What are the gaps in your knowledge and experience?
<--- Score

159. Do you have past Smart Machines successes?
<--- Score

160. What trophy do you want on your mantle?
<--- Score

161. Which individuals, teams or departments will be involved in Smart Machines?
<--- Score

162. How do you deal with Smart Machines changes?
<--- Score

163. What Smart Machines skills are most important?
<--- Score

164. What are current Smart Machines paradigms?
<--- Score

165. What will be the consequences to the stakeholder (financial, reputation etc) if Smart Machines does not go ahead or fails to deliver the objectives?
<--- Score

166. Do you say no to customers for no reason?
<--- Score

167. Do Smart Machines rules make a reasonable demand on a users capabilities?
<--- Score

168. What did you miss in the interview for the worst hire you ever made?
<--- Score

169. How are you doing compared to your industry?
<--- Score

170. Have benefits been optimized with all key stakeholders?
<--- Score

171. What was the last experiment you ran?
<--- Score

172. Why should you adopt a Smart Machines framework?
<--- Score

173. What is the purpose of Smart Machines in relation to the mission?
<--- Score

174. How can you become more high-tech but still be high touch?
<--- Score

175. How is business? Why?
<--- Score

176. What are the key enablers to make this Smart Machines move?
<--- Score

177. What is the overall business strategy?
<--- Score

178. What is your question? Why?
<--- Score

179. How do you govern and fulfill your societal responsibilities?
<--- Score

180. How will you motivate the stakeholders with the least vested interest?
<--- Score

181. Who do you think the world wants your organization to be?
<--- Score

182. If you weren't already in this business, would you enter it today? And if not, what are you going to do about it?
<--- Score

183. Among your stronger employees, how many see themselves at the company in three years? How many would leave for a 10 percent raise from another company?
<--- Score

184. Is there any existing Smart Machines governance structure?
<--- Score

185. Who is the main stakeholder, with ultimate responsibility for driving Smart Machines forward?
<--- Score

186. Who are the key stakeholders?
<--- Score

187. What is an unauthorized commitment?
<--- Score

188. Has implementation been effective in reaching specified objectives so far?
<--- Score

189. If your company went out of business tomorrow, would anyone who doesn't get a paycheck here care?
<--- Score

190. How do senior leaders deploy your organizations vision and values through your leadership system, to the workforce, to key suppliers and partners, and to customers and other stakeholders, as appropriate?
<--- Score

191. What are the essentials of internal Smart Machines management?
<--- Score

192. What are the rules and assumptions your industry operates under? What if the opposite were true?
<--- Score

193. Who will manage the integration of tools?
<--- Score

194. What have you done to protect your business from competitive encroachment?
<--- Score

195. Which models, tools and techniques are necessary?
<--- Score

196. Will there be any necessary staff changes (redundancies or new hires)?
<--- Score

197. Where can you break convention?
<--- Score

198. What would have to be true for the option on the table to be the best possible choice?
<--- Score

199. What threat is Smart Machines addressing?
<--- Score

200. Who else should you help?
<--- Score

201. Is Smart Machines dependent on the successful delivery of a current project?
<--- Score

202. Are you making progress, and are you making progress as Smart Machines leaders?
<--- Score

203. What is the range of capabilities?
<--- Score

204. Can the schedule be done in the given time?
<--- Score

205. How do you track customer value, profitability or financial return, organizational success, and sustainability?
<--- Score

206. Is the impact that Smart Machines has shown?
<--- Score

207. If no one would ever find out about your accomplishments, how would you lead differently?
<--- Score

208. Is the Smart Machines organization completing tasks effectively and efficiently?
<--- Score

209. Marketing budgets are tighter, consumers are more skeptical, and social media has changed forever the way we talk about Smart Machines. How do you gain traction?
<--- Score

210. If you got fired and a new hire took your place, what would she do different?
<--- Score

Add up total points for this section:
_____ = Total points for this section

Divided by: _____ (number of statements answered) = _____ Average score for this section

Transfer your score to the Smart Machines Index at the beginning of the Self-Assessment.

Smart Machines and Managing Projects, Criteria for Project Managers:

1.0 Initiating Process Group: Smart Machines

1. Do you understand the communication expectations for this Smart Machines project?

2. How should needs be met?

3. If the risk event occurs, what will you do?

4. How well did you do?

5. Do you know all the stakeholders impacted by the Smart Machines project and what needs are?

6. What will be the pressing issues of tomorrow?

7. How do you help others satisfy needs?

8. Just how important is your work to the overall success of the Smart Machines project?

9. What were things that you need to improve?

10. Establishment of pm office?

11. When must it be done?

12. What input will you be required to provide the Smart Machines project team?

13. Are you just doing busywork to pass the time?

14. What areas does the group agree are the biggest success on the Smart Machines project?

15. Are stakeholders properly informed about the status of the Smart Machines project?

16. Which six sigma dmaic phase focuses on why and how defects and errors occur?

17. Are you certain deliverables are properly completed and meet quality standards?

18. What were things that you did well, and could improve, and how?

19. Professionals want to know what is expected from them what are the deliverables?

20. Are there resources to maintain and support the outcome of the Smart Machines project?

1.1 Project Charter: Smart Machines

21. What is in it for you?

22. Assumptions: what factors, for planning purposes, are you considering to be true?

23. Why have you chosen the aim you have set forth?

24. Why the improvements?

25. Fit with other Products Compliments – Cannibalizes?

26. Is it an improvement over existing products?

27. Market – identify products market, including whether it is outside of the objective: what is the purpose of the program or Smart Machines project?

28. Pop quiz – which are the same inputs as in the Smart Machines project charter?

29. Review the general mission What system will be affected by the improvement efforts?

30. Why executive support?

31. What are some examples of a business case?

32. What is the business need?

33. Did your Smart Machines project ask for this?

34. Is time of the essence?

35. What are the deliverables?

36. When?

37. How high should you set your goals?

38. When will this occur?

39. Why do you manage integration?

40. Success determination factors: how will the success of the Smart Machines project be determined from the customers perspective?

1.2 Stakeholder Register: Smart Machines

41. How big is the gap?

42. What & Why?

43. Is your organization ready for change?

44. How should employers make voices heard?

45. How will reports be created?

46. How much influence do they have on the Smart Machines project?

47. Who are the stakeholders?

48. Who wants to talk about Security?

49. What is the power of the stakeholder?

50. Who is managing stakeholder engagement?

51. What are the major Smart Machines project milestones requiring communications or providing communications opportunities?

52. What opportunities exist to provide communications?

1.3 Stakeholder Analysis Matrix: Smart Machines

53. Are the required specifications for products or services changing?

54. Is there evidence that demonstrates the impact of education on the Smart Machines projects outcomes?

55. How do you manage Smart Machines project Risk?

56. How to measure the achievement of the Development Objective?

57. Global influences?

58. What do your organizations stakeholders do better than anyone else?

59. Accreditations, etc?

60. Supporters; who are the supporters?

61. Will the impacts be local, national or international?

62. Identify the stakeholders levels most frequently used –or at least sought– in your Smart Machines projects and for which purpose?

63. Seasonality, weather effects?

64. Why involve the stakeholder?

65. Sustaining internal capabilities?

66. Does your organization have bad debt or cash-flow problems?

67. Timescales, deadlines and pressures?

68. What could your organization improve?

69. Are you going to weigh the stakeholders?

70. Organizational Applicability?

71. Experience, knowledge, data?

72. Marketing - reach, distribution, awareness?

2.0 Planning Process Group: Smart Machines

73. Is the Smart Machines project supported by national and/or local organizations?

74. How will you do it?

75. To what extent do the intervention objectives and strategies of the Smart Machines project respond to your organizations plans?

76. Just how important is your work to the overall success of the Smart Machines project?

77. What is a Software Development Life Cycle (SDLC)?

78. What do they need to know about the Smart Machines project?

79. How will users learn how to use the deliverables?

80. Does it make any difference if you are successful?

81. What is the NEXT thing to do?

82. What good practices or successful experiences or transferable examples have been identified?

83. To what extent have public/private national resources and/or counterparts been mobilized to contribute to the programs objective and produce results and impacts?

84. What business situation is being addressed?

85. Do the partners have sufficient financial capacity to keep up the benefits produced by the programme?

86. How well will the chosen processes produce the expected results?

87. If action is called for, what form should it take?

88. What is the difference between the early schedule and late schedule?

89. Does the program have follow-up mechanisms (to verify the quality of the products, punctuality of delivery, etc.) to measure progress in the achievement of the envisaged results?

90. First of all, should any action be taken?

91. Is the pace of implementing the products of the program ensuring the completeness of the results of the Smart Machines project?

2.1 Project Management Plan: Smart Machines

92. What would you do differently?

93. What goes into your Smart Machines project Charter?

94. What did not work so well?

95. What went wrong?

96. Are cost risk analysis methods applied to develop contingencies for the estimated total Smart Machines project costs?

97. What are the constraints?

98. What should you drop in order to add something new?

99. Are there any client staffing expectations?

100. If the Smart Machines project is complex or scope is specialized, do you have appropriate and/or qualified staff available to perform the tasks?

101. What does management expect of PMs?

102. Will you add a schedule and diagram?

103. Is mitigation authorized or recommended?

104. Is the appropriate plan selected based on your organizations objectives and evaluation criteria expressed in Principles and Guidelines policies?

105. How do you organize the costs in the Smart Machines project management plan?

106. Do the proposed changes from the Smart Machines project include any significant risks to safety?

107. Are the existing and future without-plan conditions reasonable and appropriate?

108. Who manages integration?

109. What is Smart Machines project scope management?

110. How do you manage integration?

111. If the Smart Machines project management plan is a comprehensive document that guides you in Smart Machines project execution and control, then what should it NOT contain?

2.2 Scope Management Plan: Smart Machines

112. Do you document disagreements and work towards resolutions?

113. Has the Smart Machines project approach and development strategy of the Smart Machines project been defined, documented and accepted by the appropriate stakeholders?

114. Has the selected plan been formulated using cost effectiveness and incremental analysis techniques?

115. Have adequate resources been provided by management to ensure Smart Machines project success?

116. Has allowance been made for vacations, holidays, training (learning time for each team member), staff promotions & staff turnovers?

117. Are the payment terms being followed?

118. Will your organizations estimating methodology be used and followed?

119. Product – what are you trying to accomplish and how will you know when you are finished?

120. Are software metrics formally captured, analyzed and used as a basis for other Smart Machines project estimates?

121. Are updated Smart Machines project time & resource estimates reasonable based on the current Smart Machines project stage?

122. Process groups – where do scope management processes fit in?

123. Are you doing what you have set out to do?

124. Is there an approved case?

125. Are agendas created for each meeting with meeting objectives, meeting topics, invitee list, and action items from past meetings?

126. Are there any windfall benefits that would accrue to the Smart Machines project sponsor or other parties?

127. Does the implementation plan have an appropriate division of responsibilities?

128. Is the assigned Smart Machines project manager a PMP (Certified Smart Machines project manager) and experienced?

129. Are vendor contract reports, reviews and visits conducted periodically?

130. Are the schedule estimates reasonable given the Smart Machines project?

2.3 Requirements Management Plan: Smart Machines

131. Who will finally present the work or product(s) for acceptance?

132. To see if a requirement statement is sufficiently well-defined, read it from the developers perspective. Mentally add the phrase, call me when youre done to the end of the requirement and see if that makes you nervous. In other words, would you need additional clarification from the author to understand the requirement well enough to design and implement it?

133. What is a problem?

134. Is infrastructure setup part of your Smart Machines project?

135. What are you counting on?

136. Define the help desk model. who will take full responsibility?

137. How will you develop the schedule of requirements activities?

138. Is the system software (non-operating system) new to the IT Smart Machines project team?

139. Will you use tracing to help understand the impact of a change in requirements?

140. What performance metrics will be used?

141. Should you include sub-activities?

142. Did you avoid subjective, flowery or non-specific statements?

143. Who will do the reporting and to whom will reports be delivered?

144. What went right?

145. How will you communicate scheduled tasks to other team members?

146. Will the contractors involved take full responsibility?

147. How will requirements be managed?

148. Why manage requirements?

149. Do you understand the role that each stakeholder will play in the requirements process?

150. Which hardware or software, related to, or as outcome of the Smart Machines project is new to your organization?

2.4 Requirements Documentation: Smart Machines

151. What marketing channels do you want to use: e-mail, letter or sms?

152. What kind of entity is a problem ?

153. What is effective documentation?

154. Are there any requirements conflicts?

155. Have the benefits identified with the system being identified clearly?

156. Does your organization restrict technical alternatives?

157. Are there legal issues?

158. Who is involved?

159. The problem with gathering requirements is right there in the word gathering. What images does it conjure?

160. Can you check system requirements?

161. Basic work/business process; high-level, what is being touched?

162. How will they be documented / shared?

163. What facilities must be supported by the system?

164. Is the requirement realistically testable?

165. Is your business case still valid?

166. What is the risk associated with cost and schedule?

167. How does the proposed Smart Machines project contribute to the overall objectives of your organization?

168. What is the risk associated with the technology?

169. What is your Elevator Speech?

170. Do your constraints stand?

2.5 Requirements Traceability Matrix: Smart Machines

171. How will it affect the stakeholders personally in their career?

172. What are the chronologies, contingencies, consequences, criteria?

173. Why use a WBS?

174. How small is small enough?

175. How do you manage scope?

176. Is there a requirements traceability process in place?

177. Why do you manage scope?

178. Will you use a Requirements Traceability Matrix?

179. Do you have a clear understanding of all subcontracts in place?

180. What percentage of Smart Machines projects are producing traceability matrices between requirements and other work products?

181. Describe the process for approving requirements so they can be added to the traceability matrix and Smart Machines project work can be performed. Will the Smart Machines project requirements become

approved in writing?

182. What is the WBS?

2.6 Project Scope Statement: Smart Machines

183. Are there completion/verification criteria defined for each task producing an output?

184. Elements that deal with providing the detail?

185. Is an issue management process documented and filed?

186. How often will scope changes be reviewed?

187. Identify how your team and you will create the Smart Machines project scope statement and the work breakdown structure (WBS). Document how you will create the Smart Machines project scope statement and WBS, and make sure you answer the following questions: In defining Smart Machines project scope and the WBS, will you and your Smart Machines project team be using methods defined by your organization, methods defined by the Smart Machines project management office (PMO), or other methods?

188. Why do you need to manage scope?

189. What process would you recommend for creating the Smart Machines project scope statement?

190. If there are vendors, have they signed off on the Smart Machines project Plan?

191. Were key Smart Machines project stakeholders brought into the Smart Machines project Plan?

192. Is there a baseline plan against which to measure progress?

193. Has a method and process for requirement tracking been developed?

194. Will there be a Change Control Process in place?

195. Is the plan under configuration management?

196. Will you need a statement of work?

197. Were potential customers involved early in the planning process?

198. Who will you recommend approve the change, and when do you recommend the change reviews occur?

199. Any new risks introduced or old risks impacted. Are there issues that could affect the existing requirements for the result, service, or product if the scope changes?

200. Have you been able to thoroughly document the Smart Machines projects assumptions and constraints?

201. Will all Smart Machines project issues be unconditionally tracked through the issue resolution process?

202. Is the plan for Smart Machines project resources

adequate?

2.7 Assumption and Constraint Log: Smart Machines

203. Do the requirements meet the standards of correctness, completeness, consistency, accuracy, and readability?

204. When can log be discarded?

205. Is the definition of the Smart Machines project scope clear; what needs to be accomplished?

206. Is this process still needed?

207. What do you log?

208. Have all necessary approvals been obtained?

209. Were the system requirements formally reviewed prior to initiating the design phase?

210. Is the process working, and people are not executing in compliance of the process?

211. Have all stakeholders been identified?

212. What worked well?

213. Does a documented Smart Machines project organizational policy & plan (i.e. governance model) exist?

214. Are there processes defining how software will

be developed including development methods, overall timeline for development, software product standards, and traceability?

215. Has a Smart Machines project Communications Plan been developed?

216. Does a specific action and/or state that is known to violate security policy occur?

217. Is there documentation of system capability requirements, data requirements, environment requirements, security requirements, and computer and hardware requirements?

218. Should factors be unpredictable over time?

219. Violation trace: why ?

220. Does the system design reflect the requirements?

221. If it is out of compliance, should the process be amended or should the Plan be amended?

222. Does the document/deliverable meet general requirements (for example, statement of work) for all deliverables?

2.8 Work Breakdown Structure: Smart Machines

223. Why would you develop a Work Breakdown Structure?

224. When do you stop?

225. Who has to do it?

226. What is the probability of completing the Smart Machines project in less that xx days?

227. Do you need another level?

228. How will you and your Smart Machines project team define the Smart Machines projects scope and work breakdown structure?

229. Is it a change in scope?

230. When does it have to be done?

231. Is the work breakdown structure (wbs) defined and is the scope of the Smart Machines project clear with assigned deliverable owners?

232. When would you develop a Work Breakdown Structure?

233. What is the probability that the Smart Machines project duration will exceed xx weeks?

234. What has to be done?

235. Why is it useful?

236. How big is a work-package?

237. How many levels?

238. How far down?

239. Where does it take place?

240. Is it still viable?

241. Can you make it?

242. How much detail?

2.9 WBS Dictionary: Smart Machines

243. Does the scheduling system provide for the identification of work progress against technical and other milestones, and also provide for forecasts of completion dates of scheduled work?

244. The wbs is developed as part of a joint planning session. and how do you know that youhave done this right?

245. Are the wbs and organizational levels for application of the Smart Machines projected overhead costs identified?

246. Does the contractors system provide unit costs, equivalent unit or lot costs in terms of labor, material, other direct, and indirect costs?

247. Are estimates developed by Smart Machines project personnel coordinated with the already stated responsible for overall management to determine whether required resources will be available according to revised planning?

248. Is work progressively subdivided into detailed work packages as requirements are defined?

249. Identify and isolate causes of favorable and unfavorable cost and schedule variances?

250. Knowledgeable Smart Machines projections of future performance?

251. Identify potential or actual budget-based and time-based schedule variances?

252. Are overhead cost budgets (or Smart Machines projections) established on a facility-wide basis at least annually for the life of the contract?

253. Does the contractor require sufficient detailed planning of control accounts to constrain the application of budget initially allocated for future effort to current effort?

254. Performance to date and material commitment?

255. Does the cost accumulation system provide for summarization of indirect costs from the point of allocation to the contract total?

256. Budgets assigned to major functional organizations?

257. Is the entire contract planned in time-phased control accounts to the extent practicable?

258. Are estimates of costs at completion generated in a rational, consistent manner?

259. How detailed should a Smart Machines project get?

260. Does the contractor use objective results, design reviews and tests to trace schedule performance?

261. Does the contractors system provide for accurate cost accumulation and assignment to control accounts in a manner consistent with the budgets

using recognized acceptable costing techniques?

262. Are indirect costs accumulated for comparison with the corresponding budgets?

2.10 Schedule Management Plan: Smart Machines

263. Will the Smart Machines project sponsor be involved in preliminary schedule reviews?

264. Are scheduled deliverables actually delivered?

265. Is the ims used by all levels of management for Smart Machines project implementation and control?

266. Is a process defined to measure the performance of the schedule management process itself?

267. Are all payments made according to the contract(s)?

268. Are the processes for schedule assessment and analysis defined?

269. Are the predecessor and successor relationships accurate?

270. Have external dependencies been captured in the schedule?

271. Have the key elements of a coherent Smart Machines project management strategy been established?

272. Are the results of quality assurance reviews provided to affected groups & individuals?

273. Are there any activities or deliverables being added or gold-plated that could be dropped or scaled back without falling short of the original requirement?

274. Have all involved Smart Machines project stakeholders and work groups committed to the Smart Machines project?

275. Has the schedule been baselined?

276. Are the constraints or deadlines associated with the task accurate?

277. Have the procedures for identifying budget variances been followed?

278. Are vendor invoices audited for accuracy before payment?

279. Is it standard practice to formally commit stakeholders to the Smart Machines project via agreements?

280. Are any non-compliance issues that exist due to your organizations practices communicated to your organization?

281. Are procurement deliverables arriving on time and to specification?

282. Is quality monitored from the perspective of the customers needs and expectations?

2.11 Activity List: Smart Machines

283. How should ongoing costs be monitored to try to keep the Smart Machines project within budget?

284. What did not go as well?

285. When do the individual activities need to start and finish?

286. For other activities, how much delay can be tolerated?

287. Is infrastructure setup part of your Smart Machines project?

288. Can you determine the activity that must finish, before this activity can start?

289. In what sequence?

290. When will the work be performed?

291. How can the Smart Machines project be displayed graphically to better visualize the activities?

292. What went well?

293. What is the LF and LS for each activity?

294. What will be performed?

295. What is the probability the Smart Machines project can be completed in xx weeks?

296. How will it be performed?

297. Are the required resources available or need to be acquired?

298. How do you determine the late start (LS) for each activity?

2.12 Activity Attributes: Smart Machines

299. How do you manage time?

300. Time for overtime?

301. What is missing?

302. How difficult will it be to complete specific activities on this Smart Machines project?

303. What is the general pattern here?

304. Are the required resources available?

305. Which method produces the more accurate cost assignment?

306. Can you re-assign any activities to another resource to resolve an over-allocation?

307. What is your organizations history in doing similar activities?

308. How many resources do you need to complete the work scope within a limit of X number of days?

309. Have constraints been applied to the start and finish milestones for the phases?

310. What activity do you think you should spend the most time on?

311. Can more resources be added?

312. Why?

313. Do you feel very comfortable with your prediction?

314. Activity: what is In the Bag?

315. What conclusions/generalizations can you draw from this?

316. How else could the items be grouped?

317. Resources to accomplish the work?

2.13 Milestone List: Smart Machines

318. Can you derive how soon can the whole Smart Machines project finish?

319. Level of the Innovation?

320. Milestone pages should display the UserID of the person who added the milestone. Does a report or query exist that provides this audit information?

321. Own known vulnerabilities?

322. Which path is the critical path?

323. What would happen if a delivery of material was one week late?

324. Do you foresee any technical risks or developmental challenges?

325. How late can the activity start?

326. What background experience, skills, and strengths does the team bring to your organization?

327. What is the market for your technology, product or service?

328. Legislative effects?

329. Vital contracts and partners?

330. Information and research?

331. How difficult will it be to do specific activities on this Smart Machines project?

332. Environmental effects?

333. When will the Smart Machines project be complete?

334. Usps (unique selling points)?

2.14 Network Diagram: Smart Machines

335. What is the probability of completing the Smart Machines project in less that xx days?

336. If x is long, what would be the completion time if you break x into two parallel parts of y weeks and z weeks?

337. What activity must be completed immediately before this activity can start?

338. What can be done concurrently?

339. What to do and When?

340. What is the lowest cost to complete this Smart Machines project in xx weeks?

341. What job or jobs precede it?

342. What must be completed before an activity can be started?

343. What job or jobs could run concurrently?

344. How confident can you be in your milestone dates and the delivery date?

345. Planning: who, how long, what to do?

346. Exercise: what is the probability that the Smart

Machines project duration will exceed xx weeks?

347. If the Smart Machines project network diagram cannot change and you have extra personnel resources, what is the BEST thing to do?

348. How difficult will it be to do specific activities on this Smart Machines project?

349. What are the Key Success Factors?

350. If a current contract exists, can you provide the vendor name, contract start, and contract expiration date?

351. What controls the start and finish of a job?

352. What are the tools?

353. Where do schedules come from?

354. Where do you schedule uncertainty time?

2.15 Activity Resource Requirements: Smart Machines

355. Why do you do that?

356. Is there anything planned that does not need to be here?

357. Are there unresolved issues that need to be addressed?

358. What are constraints that you might find during the Human Resource Planning process?

359. Do you use tools like decomposition and rolling-wave planning to produce the activity list and other outputs?

360. How do you handle petty cash?

361. When does monitoring begin?

362. How many signatures do you require on a check and does this match what is in your policy and procedures?

363. Anything else?

364. What is the Work Plan Standard?

365. Other support in specific areas?

366. Which logical relationship does the PDM use

most often?

2.16 Resource Breakdown Structure: Smart Machines

367. How difficult will it be to do specific activities on this Smart Machines project?

368. How can this help you with team building?

369. Who will be used as a Smart Machines project team member?

370. Which resource planning tool provides information on resource responsibility and accountability?

371. What defines a successful Smart Machines project?

372. Who needs what information?

373. What is the primary purpose of the human resource plan?

374. Goals for the Smart Machines project. What is each stakeholders desired outcome for the Smart Machines project?

375. The list could probably go on, but, the thing that you would most like to know is, How long & How much?

376. When do they need the information?

377. Changes based on input from stakeholders?

378. What is the difference between % Complete and % work?

379. Why time management?

380. Who is allowed to see what data about which resources?

381. Which resources should be in the resource pool?

382. Is predictive resource analysis being done?

2.17 Activity Duration Estimates: Smart Machines

383. How can organizations use a weighted decision matrix to evaluate proposals as part of source selection?

384. Do you think Smart Machines project managers of large information technology Smart Machines projects need strong technical skills?

385. How does a Smart Machines project life cycle differ from a product life cycle?

386. Does a process exist to identify Smart Machines project roles, responsibilities and reporting relationships?

387. What are the three main outputs of quality control?

388. Which type of mathematical analysis is being used?

389. Are the causes of all variances identified?

390. Find an example of a contract for information technology services. Analyze the key features of the contract. What type of contract was used and why?

391. What is pmp certification, and why do you think the number of people earning it has grown so much in the past ten years?

392. How does the job market and current state of the economy affect human resource management?

393. Who will provide training for the new application?

394. What is the career outlook for Smart Machines project managers in information technology?

395. Briefly summarize the work done by Maslow, Herzberg, McClellan, McGregor, Ouchi, Thamhain and Wilemon, and Covey. How do theories relate to Smart Machines project management?

396. What is the difference between conceptual, application, and evaluative questions?

397. Which frame seemed to be the most important and why?

398. Are Smart Machines project management tools and techniques consistently applied throughout all Smart Machines projects?

399. Which would be the NEXT thing for the Smart Machines project manager to do?

400. Who will be the main sponsor for it?

401. What is the critical path for this Smart Machines project and how long is it?

2.18 Duration Estimating Worksheet: Smart Machines

402. What work will be included in the Smart Machines project?

403. Done before proceeding with this activity or what can be done concurrently?

404. What utility impacts are there?

405. What is the total time required to complete the Smart Machines project if no delays occur?

406. What is cost and Smart Machines project cost management?

407. Why estimate costs?

408. Do any colleagues have experience with your organization and/or RFPs?

409. What is an Average Smart Machines project?

410. What info is needed?

411. What is your role?

412. Can the Smart Machines project be constructed as planned?

413. When, then?

414. Small or large Smart Machines project?

415. What questions do you have?

416. Will the Smart Machines project collaborate with the local community and leverage resources?

417. How can the Smart Machines project be displayed graphically to better visualize the activities?

418. Is a construction detail attached (to aid in explanation)?

2.19 Project Schedule: Smart Machines

419. Month Smart Machines project take?

420. Smart Machines project work estimates Who is managing the work estimate quality of work tasks in the Smart Machines project schedule?

421. How effectively were issues able to be resolved without impacting the Smart Machines project Schedule or Budget?

422. What is the most mis-scheduled part of process?

423. What does that mean?

424. What is risk?

425. How can you shorten the schedule?

426. If there are any qualifying green components to this Smart Machines project, what portion of the total Smart Machines project cost is green?

427. Did the Smart Machines project come in under budget?

428. How does a Smart Machines project get to be a year late ?

429. Is infrastructure setup part of your Smart Machines project?

430. How do you know that youhave done this right?

431. Why do you need schedules?

432. Why do you need to manage Smart Machines project Risk?

433. Why is this particularly bad?

434. Why is software Smart Machines project disaster so common?

435. How can you fix it?

2.20 Cost Management Plan: Smart Machines

436. Were the budget estimates reasonable?

437. Change types and category – What are the types of changes and what are the techniques to report and control changes?

438. Is Smart Machines project status reviewed with the steering and executive teams at appropriate intervals?

439. Are there checklists created to determine if all quality processes are followed?

440. Is the structure for tracking the Smart Machines project schedule well defined and assigned to a specific individual?

441. Is the communication plan being followed?

442. Eac -estimate at completion, what is the total job expected to cost?

443. Have reserves been created to address risks?

444. What would the life cycle costs be?

445. How does the proposed individual meet each requirement?

446. Are all resource assumptions documented?

447. Best practices implementation – How will change management be applied to this Smart Machines project?

448. Are corrective actions and variances reported?

449. Is your organization certified as a supplier, wholesaler and/or regular dealer?

450. Is a stakeholder management plan in place that covers topics?

451. Was the scope definition used in task sequencing?

452. Are changes in scope (deliverable commitments) agreed to by all affected groups & individuals?

453. Has a capability assessment been conducted?

2.21 Activity Cost Estimates: Smart Machines

454. Who determines the quality and expertise of contractors?

455. In which phase of the acquisition process cycle does source qualifications reside?

456. How do you change activities?

457. What do you want to know about the stay to know if costs were inappropriately high or low?

458. Is costing method consistent with study goals?

459. What is your organizations history in doing similar tasks?

460. The impact and what actions were taken?

461. Specific - is the objective clear in terms of what, how, when, and where the situation will be changed?

462. Would you hire them again?

463. What is a Smart Machines project Management Plan?

464. How do you allocate indirect costs to activities?

465. What is Smart Machines project cost management?

466. Vac -variance at completion, how much over/under budget do you expect to be?

467. Were you satisfied with the work?

468. Is there anything unique in this Smart Machines projects scope statement that will affect resources?

469. What makes a good activity description?

470. Certification of actual expenditures?

2.22 Cost Estimating Worksheet: Smart Machines

471. Who is best positioned to know and assist in identifying corresponding factors?

472. What will others want?

473. Identify the timeframe necessary to monitor progress and collect data to determine how the selected measure has changed?

474. What happens to any remaining funds not used?

475. Value pocket identification & quantification what are value pockets?

476. Can a trend be established from historical performance data on the selected measure and are the criteria for using trend analysis or forecasting methods met?

477. What can be included?

478. Is the Smart Machines project responsive to community need?

479. What is the estimated labor cost today based upon this information?

480. Ask: are others positioned to know, are others credible, and will others cooperate?

481. How will the results be shared and to whom?

482. What costs are to be estimated?

483. Does the Smart Machines project provide innovative ways for stakeholders to overcome obstacles or deliver better outcomes?

484. Will the Smart Machines project collaborate with the local community and leverage resources?

485. What is the purpose of estimating?

486. Is it feasible to establish a control group arrangement?

487. What additional Smart Machines project(s) could be initiated as a result of this Smart Machines project?

2.23 Cost Baseline: Smart Machines

488. Is there anything unique in this Smart Machines projects scope statement that will affect resources?

489. What is the most important thing to do next to make your Smart Machines project successful?

490. Review your risk triggers -have your risks changed?

491. How accurate do cost estimates need to be?

492. Will the Smart Machines project fail if the change request is not executed?

493. Have all the product or service deliverables been accepted by the customer?

494. Has the Smart Machines project documentation been archived or otherwise disposed as described in the Smart Machines project communication plan?

495. What threats might prevent you from getting there?

496. Verify business objectives. Are others appropriate, and well-articulated?

497. What is the reality?

498. Is the cr within Smart Machines project scope?

499. What is cost and Smart Machines project cost

management?

500. Has training and knowledge transfer of the operations organization been completed?

501. Has the actual cost of the Smart Machines project (or Smart Machines project phase) been tallied and compared to the approved budget?

502. On time?

503. What is it ?

504. What does a good WBS NOT look like?

505. Who will use corresponding metrics ?

506. What do you want to measure ?

2.24 Quality Management Plan: Smart Machines

507. What are your organizations current levels and trends for the already stated measures related to customer satisfaction/ dissatisfaction and product/ service performance?

508. List your organizations customer contact standards that employees are expected to maintain. How are corresponding standards measured?

509. Show/provide copy of procedures for taking field notes?

510. Who is responsible for approving the qapp?

511. Checking the completeness and appropriateness of the sampling and testing. Were the right locations/ samples tested for the right parameters?

512. Who needs a qmp?

513. Why quality management?

514. Written by multiple authors and in multiple writing styles?

515. Is it necessary?

516. Are there trends or hot spots?

517. Do the data quality objectives communicate the

intended program need?

518. How does your organization make it easy for customers to seek assistance or complain?

519. What are the established criteria that sampling / testing data are compared against?

520. Who gets results of work?

521. When reporting to different audiences, do you vary the form or type of report?

522. You know what your customers expectations are regarding this process?

523. Are formal code reviews conducted?

524. Where do you focus?

525. Contradictory information between different documents?

526. How do senior leaders create an environment that encourages learning and innovation?

2.25 Quality Metrics: Smart Machines

527. Does risk analysis documentation meet standards?

528. Are quality metrics defined?

529. What if the biggest risk to your business were the already stated people who do not complain?

530. There are many reasons to shore up quality-related metrics, and what metrics are important?

531. What is the benchmark?

532. Has risk analysis been adequately reviewed?

533. Product Availability ?

534. How do you know if everyone is trying to improve the right things?

535. Is there a set of procedures to capture, analyze and act on quality metrics?

536. When is the security analysis testing complete?

537. Where is quality now?

538. Who is willing to lead?

539. Are there any open risk issues?

540. What are your organizations expectations for its

quality Smart Machines project?

541. How effective are your security tests?

542. What is the timeline to meet your goal?

543. Which data do others need in one place to target areas of improvement?

544. What makes a visualization memorable?

545. Subjective quality component: customer satisfaction, how do you measure it?

2.26 Process Improvement Plan: Smart Machines

546. How do you manage quality?

547. What lessons have you learned so far?

548. To elicit goal statements, do you ask a question such as, What do you want to achieve?

549. How do you measure?

550. Modeling current processes is great, and will you ever see a return on that investment?

551. What is the return on investment?

552. If a process improvement framework is being used, which elements will help the problems and goals listed?

553. Have the supporting tools been developed or acquired?

554. Why do you want to achieve the goal?

555. What personnel are the sponsors for that initiative?

556. What actions are needed to address the problems and achieve the goals?

557. Have the frequency of collection and the points

in the process where measurements will be made been determined?

558. Are you following the quality standards?

559. What personnel are the champions for the initiative?

560. Are you meeting the quality standards?

561. Management commitment at all levels?

562. Has a process guide to collect the data been developed?

563. What personnel are the change agents for your initiative?

2.27 Responsibility Assignment Matrix: Smart Machines

564. Why cost benefit analysis?

565. Not any rs, as, or cs: if an identified role is only informed, should others be eliminated from the matrix?

566. What do you need to implement earned value management?

567. Are records maintained to show how undistributed budgets are controlled?

568. What are the known stakeholder requirements?

569. Does each activity-deliverable have exactly one Accountable responsibility, so that accountability is clear and decisions can be made quickly?

570. Are your organizations and items of cost assigned to each pool identified?

571. Do you know how your people are allocated?

572. Are material costs reported within the same period as that in which BCWP is earned for that material?

573. Do work packages consist of discrete tasks which are adequately described?

574. Is work properly classified as measured effort, LOE, or apportioned effort and appropriately separated?

575. Detailed schedules which support control account and work package start and completion dates/events?

576. Contemplated overhead expenditure for each period based on the best information currently available?

577. Does the contractors system provide unit or lot costs when applicable?

578. What tool can show you individual and group allocations?

579. Are the wbs and organizational levels for application of the Smart Machines projected overhead costs identified?

580. Ideas for developing soft skills at your organization?

581. Does the contractors system include procedures for measuring the performance of critical subcontractors?

2.28 Roles and Responsibilities: Smart Machines

582. How is your work-life balance?

583. Are Smart Machines project team roles and responsibilities identified and documented?

584. What areas would you highlight for changes or improvements?

585. What expectations were met?

586. What should you do now to ensure that you are meeting all expectations of your current position?

587. Key conclusions and recommendations: Are conclusions and recommendations relevant and acceptable?

588. Accountabilities: what are the roles and responsibilities of individual team members?

589. How well did the Smart Machines project Team understand the expectations of specific roles and responsibilities?

590. What is working well within your organizations performance management system?

591. Influence: what areas of organizational decision making are you able to influence when you do not have authority to make the final decision?

592. What should you do now to prepare for your career 5+ years from now?

593. Is there a training program in place for stakeholders covering expectations, roles and responsibilities and any addition knowledge others need to be good stakeholders?

594. What areas of supervision are challenging for you?

595. What expectations were NOT met?

596. What should you do now to prepare yourself for a promotion, increased responsibilities or a different job?

597. What should you highlight for improvement?

598. Once the responsibilities are defined for the Smart Machines project, have the deliverables, roles and responsibilities been clearly communicated to every participant?

599. Concern: where are you limited or have no authority, where you can not influence?

600. Are governance roles and responsibilities documented?

601. Do you take the time to clearly define roles and responsibilities on Smart Machines project tasks?

2.29 Human Resource Management Plan: Smart Machines

602. Is the manpower level sufficient to meet the future business requirements?

603. Are post milestone Smart Machines project reviews (PMPR) conducted with your organization at least once a year?

604. Do Smart Machines project managers participating in the Smart Machines project know the Smart Machines projects true status first hand?

605. Is it standard practice to formally commit stakeholders to the Smart Machines project via agreements?

606. Does the detailed work plan match the complexity of tasks with the capabilities of personnel?

607. Are the appropriate IT resources adequate to meet planned commitments?

608. Are people motivated to meet the current and future challenges?

609. Have the key elements of a coherent Smart Machines project management strategy been established?

610. Have key stakeholders been identified?

611. Have activity relationships and interdependencies within tasks been adequately identified?

612. Are staff skills known and available for each task?

613. Is the structure for tracking the Smart Machines project schedule well defined and assigned to a specific individual?

614. How will the Smart Machines project manage expectations & meet needs and requirements?

615. Is the schedule updated on a periodic basis?

616. Have Smart Machines project management standards and procedures been identified / established and documented?

2.30 Communications Management Plan: Smart Machines

617. Who will use or be affected by the result of a Smart Machines project?

618. Will messages be directly related to the release strategy or phases of the Smart Machines project?

619. How were corresponding initiatives successful?

620. Which team member will work with each stakeholder?

621. Are others part of the communications management plan?

622. In your work, how much time is spent on stakeholder identification?

623. Which stakeholders can influence others?

624. Why do you manage communications?

625. Do you then often overlook a key stakeholder or stakeholder group?

626. What does the stakeholder need from the team?

627. What is the stakeholders level of authority?

628. Are stakeholders internal or external?

629. Where do team members get information?

630. What data is going to be required?

631. Do you feel more overwhelmed by stakeholders?

632. Who is responsible?

633. Why manage stakeholders?

634. What steps can you take for a positive relationship?

635. How will the person responsible for executing the communication item be notified?

636. Are there potential barriers between the team and the stakeholder?

2.31 Risk Management Plan: Smart Machines

637. Does the customer understand the software process?

638. Market risk: will the new product be useful to your organization or marketable to others?

639. Do you have a consistent repeatable process that is actually used?

640. What is the likelihood?

641. Mitigation -how can you avoid the risk?

642. What will drive change?

643. Premium on reliability of product?

644. What is the impact to the Smart Machines project if the item is not resolved in a timely fashion?

645. What should be done with non-critical risks?

646. My Smart Machines project leader has suddenly left your organization, what do you do?

647. For software; are compilers and code generators available and suitable for the product to be built?

648. Who should be notified of the occurrence of each of the indicators?

649. Technology risk: is the Smart Machines project technically feasible?

650. Are status updates being made on schedule and are the updates clearly described?

651. Are formal technical reviews part of this process?

652. How risk averse are you?

653. Market risk -will the new service or product be useful to your organization or marketable to others?

654. User involvement: do you have the right users?

655. Minimize cost and financial risk?

656. Are tools for analysis and design available?

2.32 Risk Register: Smart Machines

657. Does the evidence highlight any areas to advance opportunities or foster good relations. If yes what steps will be taken?

658. What are the assumptions and current status that support the assessment of the risk?

659. Are there any knock-on effects/impact on any of the other areas?

660. What is a Community Risk Register?

661. What has changed since the last period?

662. Preventative actions - planned actions to reduce the likelihood a risk will occur and/or reduce the seriousness should it occur. What should you do now?

663. Cost/benefit – how much will the proposed mitigations cost and how does this cost compare with the potential cost of the risk event/situation should it occur?

664. Are corrective measures implemented as planned?

665. Contingency actions - planned actions to reduce the immediate seriousness of the risk when it does occur. What should you do when?

666. What are you going to do to limit the Smart Machines projects risk exposure due to the identified

risks?

667. How is a Community Risk Register created?

668. Can the likelihood and impact of failing to achieve corresponding recommendations and action plans be assessed?

669. Methodology: how will risk management be performed on this Smart Machines project?

670. What is your current and future risk profile?

671. What could prevent you delivering on the strategic program objectives and what is being done to mitigate corresponding issues?

672. People risk -are people with appropriate skills available to help complete the Smart Machines project?

673. Technology risk -is the Smart Machines project technically feasible?

674. What evidence do you have to justify the likelihood score of the risk (audit, incident report, claim, complaints, inspection, internal review)?

675. What is the reason for current performance gaps and do the risks and opportunities identified previously account for this?

2.33 Probability and Impact Assessment: Smart Machines

676. Are flexibility and reuse paramount?

677. How realistic is the timing of introduction?

678. Do the people have the right combinations of skills?

679. Prioritized components/features?

680. Can it be enlarged by drawing people from other areas of your organization?

681. Can you avoid altogether some things that might go wrong?

682. Is the Smart Machines project cutting across the entire organization?

683. Management -what contingency plans do you have if the risk becomes a reality?

684. Who should be notified of the occurrence of each of the risk indicators?

685. What is the past performance of the Smart Machines project manager?

686. What will be the impact or consequence if the risk occurs?

687. What risks does your organization have if the Smart Machines projects fail to meet deadline?

688. Do you use diagramming techniques to show cause and effect?

689. Which of your Smart Machines projects should be selected when compared with other Smart Machines projects?

690. Do you manage the process through use of metrics?

691. What are the levels of understanding of the future users of the outcome/results of this Smart Machines project?

692. Can this technology be absorbed with current level of expertise available in your organization?

693. Have customers been involved fully in the definition of requirements?

2.34 Probability and Impact Matrix: Smart Machines

694. What would be the best solution?

695. Have staff received necessary training?

696. What are the current requirements of the customer?

697. What would be the effect of slippage?

698. What do you expect?

699. Is the present organizational structure for handling the Smart Machines project sufficient?

700. Who is going to be the consortium leader?

701. Lay ground work for future returns?

702. Is Smart Machines project scope stable?

703. What are data sources?

704. What things might go wrong?

705. Can the risk be avoided by choosing a different alternative?

706. Could others have been better mitigated?

707. What are the preparations required for facing

difficulties?

708. How should you structure risks?

709. What is the likelihood of a breakthrough?

710. Were there any Smart Machines projects similar to this one in existence?

711. What will the damage be?

712. What is the probability of the risk occurring?

713. Is security a central objective?

2.35 Risk Data Sheet: Smart Machines

714. What were the Causes that contributed?

715. How can it happen?

716. Who has a vested interest in how you perform as your organization (our stakeholders)?

717. Potential for recurrence?

718. What was measured?

719. During work activities could hazards exist?

720. Type of risk identified?

721. What do you know?

722. What can happen?

723. How do you handle product safely?

724. What if client refuses?

725. What are the main opportunities available to you that you should grab while you can?

726. What is the environment within which you operate (social trends, economic, community values, broad based participation, national directions etc.)?

727. What is the chance that it will happen?

728. If it happens, what are the consequences?

729. What is the duration of infection (the length of time the host is infected with the organizm) in a normal healthy human host?

730. Do effective diagnostic tests exist?

731. What are you trying to achieve (Objectives)?

732. How reliable is the data source?

733. What can you do?

2.36 Procurement Management Plan: Smart Machines

734. Are updated Smart Machines project time & resource estimates reasonable based on the current Smart Machines project stage?

735. Are stakeholders aware and supportive of the principles and practices of modern software estimation?

736. Are Smart Machines project team roles and responsibilities identified and documented?

737. Is there a procurement management plan in place?

738. Do Smart Machines project managers participating in the Smart Machines project know the Smart Machines projects true status first hand?

739. Financial capacity; does the seller have, or can the seller reasonably be expected to obtain, the financial resources needed?

740. Does all Smart Machines project documentation reside in a common repository for easy access?

741. Does the Smart Machines project have a Quality Culture?

742. Does the schedule include Smart Machines project management time and change request

analysis time?

743. Smart Machines project Objectives?

744. Are cause and effect determined for risks when others occur?

745. Are risk triggers captured?

746. Are actuals compared against estimates to analyze and correct variances?

747. Have stakeholder accountabilities & responsibilities been clearly defined?

748. What communication items need improvement?

2.37 Source Selection Criteria: Smart Machines

749. Can you identify proposed teaming partners and/or subcontractors and consider the nature and extent of proposed involvement in satisfying the Smart Machines project requirements?

750. What is the last item a Smart Machines project manager must do to finalize Smart Machines project close-out?

751. What documentation is needed for a tradeoff decision?

752. What past performance information should be requested?

753. How do you encourage efficiency and consistency?

754. Will the technical evaluation factor unnecessarily force the acquisition into a higher-priced market segment?

755. Is experience evaluated?

756. Are resultant proposal revisions allowed?

757. How do you ensure an integrated assessment of proposals?

758. Do you prepare an independent cost estimate?

759. What information may not be provided?

760. In the technical/management area, what criteria do you use to determine the final evaluation ratings?

761. How should the preproposal conference be conducted?

762. Are types/quantities of material, facilities appropriate?

763. How much weight should be placed on past performance information?

764. Is the offeror pricing what is technically proposed?

765. Do you want to have them collaborate at subfactor level?

766. What should preproposal conferences accomplish?

767. Do you have designated specific forms or worksheets?

768. How do you consolidate reviews and analysis of evaluators?

2.38 Stakeholder Management Plan: Smart Machines

769. Who is responsible for gathering and reporting data for employment?

770. Are internal Smart Machines project status meetings held at reasonable intervals?

771. Do you use diagrams and tables to account for complex concepts and increase overall readability?

772. In your opinion, do certain Smart Machines project resources hold a higher importance than other resources?

773. Who will be responsible for managing and maintaining the Issues Register?

774. What methods are to be used for managing and monitoring subcontractors (eg agreements, contracts etc)?

775. Was your organizations estimating methodology being used and followed?

776. Who would sign off on the charter?

777. Are the quality tools and methods identified in the Quality Plan appropriate to the Smart Machines project?

778. Are risk oriented checklists used during risk

identification?

779. Are Smart Machines project contact logs kept up to date?

780. What are the criteria for selecting suppliers of off the shelf products?

781. Has a provision been made to reassess Smart Machines project risks at various Smart Machines project stages?

782. What potential impact does the stakeholder have on the Smart Machines project?

783. Does the plan conform to standards?

784. Pareto diagrams, statistical sampling, flow charting or trend analysis used quality monitoring?

785. What are the advantages and disadvantages of using external contracted resources?

786. What procedures will be utilised to ensure effective monitoring of Smart Machines project progress?

2.39 Change Management Plan: Smart Machines

787. Are work location changes required?

788. What is the worst thing that can happen if you communicate information?

789. What is the most cynical response it can receive?

790. What is the most positive interpretation it can receive?

791. Is there a need for new relationships to be built?

792. Has the training provider been established?

793. When to start change management?

794. Will the culture embrace or reject this change?

795. Has a training need analysis been carried out?

796. Who might be able to help you the most?

797. What new behaviours are required?

798. What does a resilient organization look like?

799. What time commitment will this involve?

800. What will be the preferred method of delivery?

801. How frequently should you repeat the message?

802. What roles within your organization are affected, and how?

803. What goal(s) do you hope to accomplish?

804. What would be an estimate of the total cost for the activities required to carry out the change initiative?

805. What is the worst thing that can happen if you chose not to communicate this information?

3.0 Executing Process Group: Smart Machines

806. What type of people would you want on your team?

807. Will new hardware or software be required for servers or client machines?

808. What is in place for ensuring adequate change control on Smart Machines projects that involve outside contracts?

809. How well did the team follow the chosen processes?

810. After how many days will the lease cost be the same as the purchase cost for the equipment?

811. How will you avoid scope creep?

812. Do your results resemble a normal distribution?

813. Will additional funds be needed for hardware or software?

814. How well did the chosen processes fit the needs of the Smart Machines project?

815. In what way has the program come up with innovative measures for problem-solving?

816. Is activity definition the first process involved in

Smart Machines project time management?

817. How many different communication channels does the Smart Machines project team have?

818. When is the appropriate time to bring the scorecard to Board meetings?

819. Is the Smart Machines project performing better or worse than planned?

820. Would you rate yourself as being risk-averse, risk-neutral, or risk-seeking?

821. Does the case present a realistic scenario?

822. What are the main types of goods and services being outsourced?

823. How do you prevent staff are just doing busywork to pass the time?

824. Will outside resources be needed to help?

3.1 Team Member Status Report: Smart Machines

825. Will the staff do training or is that done by a third party?

826. Are the products of your organizations Smart Machines projects meeting customers objectives?

827. How much risk is involved?

828. Are your organizations Smart Machines projects more successful over time?

829. Is there evidence that staff is taking a more professional approach toward management of your organizations Smart Machines projects?

830. Why is it to be done?

831. Does your organization have the means (staff, money, contract, etc.) to produce or to acquire the product, good, or service?

832. What specific interest groups do you have in place?

833. Are the attitudes of staff regarding Smart Machines project work improving?

834. Do you have an Enterprise Smart Machines project Management Office (EPMO)?

835. How will resource planning be done?

836. How it is to be done?

837. What is to be done?

838. How does this product, good, or service meet the needs of the Smart Machines project and your organization as a whole?

839. The problem with Reward & Recognition Programs is that the truly deserving people all too often get left out. How can you make it practical?

840. Does the product, good, or service already exist within your organization?

841. How can you make it practical?

842. When a teams productivity and success depend on collaboration and the efficient flow of information, what generally fails them?

843. Does every department have to have a Smart Machines project Manager on staff?

3.2 Change Request: Smart Machines

844. How does a team identify the discrete elements of a configuration?

845. What should be regulated in a change control operating instruction?

846. Should a more thorough impact analysis be conducted?

847. Who is included in the change control team?

848. Who needs to approve change requests?

849. How many lines of code must be changed to implement the change?

850. Will new change requests be acknowledged in a timely manner?

851. How are changes requested (forms, method of communication)?

852. Is it feasible to use requirements attributes as predictors of reliability?

853. How is quality being addressed on the Smart Machines project?

854. Describe how modifications, enhancements, defects and/or deficiencies shall be notified (e.g. Problem Reports, Change Requests etc) and managed. Detail warranty and/or maintenance

periods?

855. What kind of information about the change request needs to be captured?

856. When do you create a change request?

857. Are there requirements attributes that are strongly related to the occurrence of defects and failures?

858. What needs to be communicated?

859. What is the relationship between requirements attributes and reliability?

860. Can static requirements change attributes like the size of the change be used to predict reliability in execution?

861. Since there are no change requests in your Smart Machines project at this point, what must you have before you begin?

862. What is a Change Request Form?

863. Who can suggest changes?

3.3 Change Log: Smart Machines

864. How does this change affect scope?

865. Is the change request within Smart Machines project scope?

866. Do the described changes impact on the integrity or security of the system?

867. Is the change backward compatible without limitations?

868. Where do changes come from?

869. Is this a mandatory replacement?

870. How does this relate to the standards developed for specific business processes?

871. Is the requested change request a result of changes in other Smart Machines project(s)?

872. Is the submitted change a new change or a modification of a previously approved change?

873. Does the suggested change request represent a desired enhancement to the products functionality?

874. Is the change request open, closed or pending?

875. When was the request approved?

876. How does this change affect the timeline of the

schedule?

877. Does the suggested change request seem to represent a necessary enhancement to the product?

878. Who initiated the change request?

879. When was the request submitted?

880. Will the Smart Machines project fail if the change request is not executed?

3.4 Decision Log: Smart Machines

881. Which variables make a critical difference?

882. What is your overall strategy for quality control / quality assurance procedures?

883. What was the rationale for the decision?

884. How does an increasing emphasis on cost containment influence the strategies and tactics used?

885. What alternatives/risks were considered?

886. Who is the decisionmaker?

887. Meeting purpose; why does this team meet?

888. Decision-making process; how will the team make decisions?

889. With whom was the decision shared or considered?

890. At what point in time does loss become unacceptable?

891. Behaviors; what are guidelines that the team has identified that will assist them with getting the most out of team meetings?

892. How do you define success?

893. How consolidated and comprehensive a story can you tell by capturing currently available incident data in a central location and through a log of key decisions during an incident?

894. Who will be given a copy of this document and where will it be kept?

895. Is your opponent open to a non-traditional workflow, or will it likely challenge anything you do?

896. Linked to original objective?

897. What makes you different or better than others companies selling the same thing?

898. How does the use a Decision Support System influence the strategies/tactics or costs?

899. How effective is maintaining the log at facilitating organizational learning?

900. Does anything need to be adjusted?

3.5 Quality Audit: Smart Machines

901. Do the acceptance procedures and specifications include the criteria for acceptance/rejection, define the process to be used, and specify the measuring and test equipment that is to be used?

902. What data about organizational performance is routinely collected and reported?

903. Are people allowed to contribute ideas?

904. How does your organization know that its system for ensuring that its training activities are appropriately resourced and support is appropriately effective and constructive?

905. Does your organization have set of goals, objectives, strategies and targets that are clearly understood by the Board and staff?

906. How does your organization know that its planning processes are appropriately effective and constructive?

907. Are there sufficient personnel having the necessary education, background, training, and experience to assure that all operations are correctly performed?

908. How does your organization know that its staff placements are appropriately effective and constructive in relation to program-related learning outcomes?

909. How does your organization know that its methods are appropriately effective and constructive?

910. What does an analysis of your organizations staff profile suggest in terms of its planning, and how is this being addressed?

911. Is your organizational structure established and each positions responsibility defined?

912. How does your organization know that its public relations and marketing systems are appropriately effective and constructive?

913. What mechanisms exist for identification of staff development needs?

914. Is the process of self review, learning and improvement endemic throughout your organization?

915. How does your organization know that the support for its staff is appropriately effective and constructive?

916. How does your organization know that its management of its ethical responsibilities is appropriately effective and constructive?

917. How does your organization know that its relationships with industry and employers are appropriately effective and constructive?

918. How does your organization know that its management system is appropriately effective and

constructive?

919. How does your organization know that its system for governing staff behaviour is appropriately effective and constructive?

3.6 Team Directory: Smart Machines

920. Process decisions: do job conditions warrant additional actions to collect job information and document on-site activity?

921. Where will the product be used and/or delivered or built when appropriate?

922. Who should receive information (all stakeholders)?

923. Who is the Sponsor?

924. Who will be the stakeholders on your next Smart Machines project?

925. Why is the work necessary?

926. Where should the information be distributed?

927. Do purchase specifications and configurations match requirements?

928. Process decisions: which organizational elements and which individuals will be assigned management functions?

929. Does a Smart Machines project team directory list all resources assigned to the Smart Machines project?

930. How will the team handle changes?

931. How will you accomplish and manage the objectives?

932. Process decisions: is work progressing on schedule and per contract requirements?

933. Who are your stakeholders (customers, sponsors, end users, team members)?

934. Timing: when do the effects of communication take place?

935. How and in what format should information be presented?

936. Process decisions: are all start-up, turn over and close out requirements of the contract satisfied?

937. Who will talk to the customer?

938. Have you decided when to celebrate the Smart Machines projects completion date?

939. How do unidentified risks impact the outcome of the Smart Machines project?

3.7 Team Operating Agreement: Smart Machines

940. Reimbursements: how will the team members be reimbursed for expenses and time commitments?

941. Do you ensure that all participants know how to use the required technology?

942. What is group supervision?

943. Do you vary your voice pace, tone and pitch to engage participants and gain involvement?

944. Are leadership responsibilities shared among team members (versus a single leader)?

945. Are there influences outside the team that may affect performance, and if so, have you identified and addressed them?

946. Do you ask participants to close laptops and place mobile devices on silent on the table while the meeting is in progress?

947. Do you send out the agenda and meeting materials in advance?

948. Have you established procedures that team members can follow to work effectively together, such as a team operating agreement?

949. Do you brief absent members after they view

meeting notes or listen to a recording?

950. Are there more than two native languages represented by your team?

951. The method to be used in the decision making process; Will it be consensus, majority rule, or the supervisor having the final say?

952. What is your unique contribution to your organization?

953. How will group handle unplanned absences?

954. Do you begin with a question to engage everyone?

955. What are the boundaries (organizational or geographic) within which you operate?

956. What are some potential sources of conflict among team members?

957. What administrative supports will be put in place to support the team and the teams supervisor?

958. Are team roles clearly defined and accepted?

959. Do you solicit member feedback about meetings and what would make them better?

3.8 Team Performance Assessment: Smart Machines

960. If you are worried about method variance before you collect data, what sort of design elements might you include to reduce or eliminate the threat of method variance?

961. To what degree are fresh input and perspectives systematically caught and added (for example, through information and analysis, new members, and senior sponsors)?

962. If you have criticized someones work for method variance in your role as reviewer, what was the circumstance?

963. How do you manage human resources?

964. How hard do you try to make a good selection?

965. How much interpersonal friction is there in your team?

966. To what degree do team members feel that the purpose of the team is important, if not exciting?

967. How do you recognize and praise members for contributions?

968. To what degree does the teams approach to its work allow for modification and improvement over time?

969. Effects of crew composition on crew performance: Does the whole equal the sum of its parts?

970. What are teams?

971. Do you give group members authority to make at least some important decisions?

972. To what degree are staff involved as partners in the improvement process?

973. To what degree do all members feel responsible for all agreed-upon measures?

974. To what degree do team members agree with the goals, relative importance, and the ways in which achievement will be measured?

975. To what degree can team members meet frequently enough to accomplish the teams ends?

976. Social categorization and intergroup behaviour: Does minimal intergroup discrimination make social identity more positive?

977. To what degree does the teams work approach provide opportunity for members to engage in fact-based problem solving?

978. Is there a particular method of data analysis that you would recommend as a means of demonstrating that method variance is not of great concern for a given dataset?

979. To what degree does the teams purpose constitute a broader, deeper aspiration than just accomplishing short-term goals?

3.9 Team Member Performance Assessment: Smart Machines

980. Are the goals SMART ?

981. To what degree do team members articulate the teams work approach?

982. How do you currently use the time that is available?

983. To what degree are sub-teams possible or necessary?

984. Should a ratee get a copy of all the raters documents about the employees performance?

985. For what period of time is a member rated?

986. Verify business objectives. Are they appropriate, and well-articulated?

987. How do you make use of research?

988. What stakeholders must be involved in the development and oversight of the performance plan?

989. How is your organizations Strategic Management System tied to performance measurement?

990. How do you currently account for your results in the teams achievement?

991. To what degree can all members engage in open and interactive considerations?

992. Has the appropriate access to relevant data and analysis capability been granted?

993. How are training activities developed from a technical perspective?

994. What innovations (if any) are developed to realize goals?

995. What are acceptable governance changes?

996. What tools are available to determine whether all contract functional and compliance areas of performance objectives, measures, and incentives have been met?

997. What is the large, desired outcome?

3.10 Issue Log: Smart Machines

998. Persistence; will users learn a work around or will they be bothered every time?

999. Who were proponents/opponents?

1000. What is a Stakeholder?

1001. Are there too many who have an interest in some aspect of your work?

1002. Who do you turn to if you have questions?

1003. In classifying stakeholders, which approach to do so are you using?

1004. Who is the issue assigned to?

1005. Do you feel a register helps?

1006. What are the typical contents?

1007. Can you think of other people who might have concerns or interests?

1008. What are the stakeholders interrelationships?

1009. Who needs to know and how much?

1010. Do you prepare stakeholder engagement plans?

1011. Which stakeholders are thought leaders, influences, or early adopters?

1012. What would have to change?

4.0 Monitoring and Controlling Process Group: Smart Machines

1013. What is the expected monetary value of the Smart Machines project?

1014. Who needs to be involved in the planning?

1015. Change, where should you look for problems?

1016. What do they need to know about the Smart Machines project?

1017. Measurable - are the targets measurable?

1018. Is the program making progress in helping to achieve the set results?

1019. How were collaborations developed, and how are they sustained?

1020. Overall, how does the program function to serve the clients?

1021. What resources are necessary?

1022. Did you implement the program as designed?

1023. User: who wants the information and what are they interested in?

1024. Is there adequate validation on required fields?

1025. How are you doing?

1026. Did the Smart Machines project team have the right skills?

1027. What were things that you did very well and want to do the same again on the next Smart Machines project?

1028. What input will you be required to provide the Smart Machines project team?

4.1 Project Performance Report: Smart Machines

1029. To what degree does the team possess adequate membership to achieve its ends?

1030. To what degree does the information network communicate information relevant to the task?

1031. What is the degree to which rules govern information exchange between individuals within your organization?

1032. How will procurement be coordinated with other Smart Machines project aspects, such as scheduling and performance reporting?

1033. To what degree does the teams work approach provide opportunity for members to engage in open interaction?

1034. To what degree does the formal organization make use of individual resources and meet individual needs?

1035. To what degree do team members understand one anothers roles and skills?

1036. To what degree are the demands of the task compatible with and converge with the mission and functions of the formal organization?

1037. To what degree can the cognitive capacity of

individuals accommodate the flow of information?

1038. To what degree are the tasks requirements reflected in the flow and storage of information?

1039. To what degree do team members frequently explore the teams purpose and its implications?

1040. To what degree can the team ensure that all members are individually and jointly accountable for the teams purpose, goals, approach, and work-products?

1041. To what degree can the team measure progress against specific goals?

1042. To what degree does the teams work approach provide opportunity for members to engage in results-based evaluation?

1043. To what degree is there centralized control of information sharing?

1044. To what degree are the demands of the task compatible with and converge with the relationships of the informal organization?

4.2 Variance Analysis: Smart Machines

1045. Is the market likely to continue to grow at this rate next year?

1046. Who are responsible for overhead performance control of related costs?

1047. Is budgeted cost for work performed calculated in a manner consistent with the way work is planned?

1048. Can the contractor substantiate work package and planning package budgets?

1049. Are all authorized tasks assigned to identified organizational elements?

1050. How do you manage changes in the nature of the overhead requirements?

1051. Does the contractors system identify work accomplishment against the schedule plan?

1052. What is the expected future profitability of each customer?

1053. Did your organization lose existing customers and/or gain new customers?

1054. Are all cwbs elements specified for external reporting?

1055. How does your organization allocate the cost of shared expenses and services?

1056. Are the bases and rates for allocating costs from each indirect pool consistently applied?

1057. Favorable or unfavorable variance?

1058. Are the requirements for all items of overhead established by rational, traceable processes?

1059. How do you evaluate the impact of schedule changes, work around, et?

1060. Are detailed work packages planned as far in advance as practicable?

1061. Is there a logical explanation for any variance?

1062. What is the total budget for the Smart Machines project (including estimates for authorized and unpriced work)?

4.3 Earned Value Status: Smart Machines

1063. Are you hitting your Smart Machines projects targets?

1064. Verification is a process of ensuring that the developed system satisfies the stakeholders agreements and specifications; Are you building the product right? What do you haverify?

1065. Where is evidence-based earned value in your organization reported?

1066. If earned value management (EVM) is so good in determining the true status of a Smart Machines project and Smart Machines project its completion, why is it that hardly any one uses it in information systems related Smart Machines projects?

1067. When is it going to finish?

1068. Validation is a process of ensuring that the developed system will actually achieve the stakeholders desired outcomes; Are you building the right product? What do you validate?

1069. How much is it going to cost by the finish?

1070. Earned value can be used in almost any Smart Machines project situation and in almost any Smart Machines project environment. it may be used on large Smart Machines projects, medium sized Smart

Machines projects, tiny Smart Machines projects (in cut-down form), complex and simple Smart Machines projects and in any market sector. some people, of course, know all about earned value, they have used it for years - but perhaps not as effectively as they could have?

1071. How does this compare with other Smart Machines projects?

1072. What is the unit of forecast value?

1073. Where are your problem areas?

4.4 Risk Audit: Smart Machines

1074. Where will the next scandal or adverse media involving your organization come from?

1075. Is safety information provided to all involved?

1076. Do you have written and signed agreements/contracts in place for each paid staff member?

1077. Are all managers or operators of the facility or equipment competent or qualified?

1078. Do you record and file all audits?

1079. Does the team have the right mix of skills?

1080. What are risks and how do you manage them?

1081. What are the differences and similarities between strategic and operational risks in your organization?

1082. Are staff committed for the duration of the product?

1083. Is the customer willing to establish rapid communication links with the developer?

1084. What expertise do auditors need to generate effective business-level risk assessments, and to what extent do auditors currently possess the already stated attributes?

1085. Are enough people available?

1086. Are the best people available?

1087. Are you willing to seek legal advice when required?

1088. Have all possible risks/hazards been identified (including injury to staff, damage to equipment, impact on others in the community)?

1089. Does your board meet regularly and document all decisions and actions?

1090. The halo effect in business risk audits: can strategic risk assessment bias auditor judgment about accounting details?

1091. Have risks been considered with an insurance broker or provider and suitable insurance cover been arranged?

1092. Are you aware of the industry standards that apply to your operations?

1093. Do you meet the legislative requirements (for example PAYG, super contributions) for paid employees?

4.5 Contractor Status Report: Smart Machines

1094. What was the actual budget or estimated cost for your organizations services?

1095. Are there contractual transfer concerns?

1096. What was the budget or estimated cost for your organizations services?

1097. What is the average response time for answering a support call?

1098. What was the final actual cost?

1099. What are the minimum and optimal bandwidth requirements for the proposed soluiton?

1100. Who can list a Smart Machines project as organization experience, your organization or a previous employee of your organization?

1101. Describe how often regular updates are made to the proposed solution. Are corresponding regular updates included in the standard maintenance plan?

1102. What process manages the contracts?

1103. What was the overall budget or estimated cost?

1104. If applicable; describe your standard schedule for new software version releases. Are new software version releases included in the standard maintenance plan?

1105. How long have you been using the services?

1106. How is risk transferred?

4.6 Formal Acceptance: Smart Machines

1107. How does your team plan to obtain formal acceptance on your Smart Machines project?

1108. Do you buy-in installation services?

1109. Was the Smart Machines project goal achieved?

1110. How well did the team follow the methodology?

1111. Did the Smart Machines project manager and team act in a professional and ethical manner?

1112. What is the Acceptance Management Process?

1113. Who would use it?

1114. Was business value realized?

1115. What function(s) does it fill or meet?

1116. Did the Smart Machines project achieve its MOV?

1117. Was the sponsor/customer satisfied?

1118. Was the Smart Machines project managed well?

1119. Who supplies data?

1120. What features, practices, and processes proved

to be strengths or weaknesses?

1121. What was done right?

1122. Does it do what client said it would?

1123. What can you do better next time?

1124. Do you perform formal acceptance or burn-in tests?

1125. Was the Smart Machines project work done on time, within budget, and according to specification?

1126. Does it do what Smart Machines project team said it would?

5.0 Closing Process Group: Smart Machines

1127. What will you do?

1128. What will you do to minimize the impact should a risk event occur?

1129. How well did the chosen processes fit the needs of the Smart Machines project?

1130. Did the Smart Machines project team have enough people to execute the Smart Machines project plan?

1131. What could have been improved?

1132. What level of risk does the proposed budget represent to the Smart Machines project?

1133. Did you do what you said you were going to do?

1134. What is the overall risk of the Smart Machines project to your organization?

1135. What areas were overlooked on this Smart Machines project?

1136. What is an Encumbrance?

1137. Who are the Smart Machines project stakeholders?

1138. Were the outcomes different from the already stated planned?

1139. What is the Smart Machines project name and date of completion?

1140. Were escalated issues resolved promptly?

1141. What is the risk of failure to your organization?

1142. How will staff learn how to use the deliverables?

5.1 Procurement Audit: Smart Machines

1143. Are the journals and ledgers kept current for all funds?

1144. Is the performance of the procurement function/unit benchmarked with other procurement functions/units in the different stages of the procurement process?

1145. Were no tenders presented after the time limit accepted?

1146. Are there mechanisms in place to evaluate the performance of the departments suppliers?

1147. Does the procurement Smart Machines project have a clear goal and does the goal meet the specified needs of the users?

1148. Who are the key suppliers?

1149. Is there a system in place to handle partial delivery of orders, back orders, and partial payments?

1150. Is there time waste during tendering?

1151. Was the chosen procedure the most efficient and effective for the performance of the contract?

1152. Are all purchase orders cancelled after payment to avoid duplicate payment of the same invoice?

1153. Are behaviour modification applied to change procurement of goods and services if procurement is not functioning properly?

1154. Were additional works strictly necessary for the completion of performance under the contract?

1155. Are checks disbursed by someone other than the individual who authorized payment?

1156. Were any additional works or deliveries admissible without the need for a new procurement procedure?

1157. Are there performance targets on value for money obtained and cost savings?

1158. Are buyers rotated so that they do not deal with the same vendors year in and year out?

1159. Are open purchase orders with a fixed monetary limitation used for local purchases of small dollar value?

1160. Is the routing of copies of purchase order forms defined?

1161. Do procedures require cash advances to be returned by transferred or terminated employees before they can receive final paychecks?

1162. Are there complementary rules to be used and are they applied?

5.2 Contract Close-Out: Smart Machines

1163. Was the contract type appropriate?

1164. What is capture management?

1165. Parties: Authorized?

1166. Have all contracts been completed?

1167. How/when used ?

1168. Have all acceptance criteria been met prior to final payment to contractors?

1169. Parties: who is involved?

1170. Why Outsource?

1171. Are the signers the authorized officials?

1172. Have all contracts been closed?

1173. Was the contract complete without requiring numerous changes and revisions?

1174. Change in attitude or behavior?

1175. Change in circumstances?

1176. How is the contracting office notified of the automatic contract close-out?

1177. Change in knowledge?

1178. Have all contract records been included in the Smart Machines project archives?

1179. What happens to the recipient of services?

1180. Was the contract sufficiently clear so as not to result in numerous disputes and misunderstandings?

1181. How does it work?

1182. Has each contract been audited to verify acceptance and delivery?

5.3 Project or Phase Close-Out: Smart Machines

1183. Did the delivered product meet the specified requirements and goals of the Smart Machines project?

1184. What security considerations needed to be addressed during the procurement life cycle?

1185. What are the informational communication needs for each stakeholder?

1186. Does the lesson educate others to improve performance?

1187. What information is each stakeholder group interested in?

1188. Who controlled the resources for the Smart Machines project?

1189. What was expected from each stakeholder?

1190. What can you do better next time, and what specific actions can you take to improve?

1191. Who is responsible for award close-out?

1192. Who controlled key decisions that were made?

1193. What were the actual outcomes?

1194. In preparing the Lessons Learned report, should it reflect a consensus viewpoint, or should the report reflect the different individual viewpoints?

1195. What information did each stakeholder need to contribute to the Smart Machines projects success?

1196. What was learned?

1197. Were cost budgets met?

1198. Planned remaining costs?

1199. What is the information level of detail required for each stakeholder?

1200. Planned completion date?

5.4 Lessons Learned: Smart Machines

1201. How useful and complete was the Smart Machines project document repository?

1202. How effective were the techniques used to prepare you and your organization for the impact of the changes brought about by the product or service produced by the Smart Machines project?

1203. How useful was your testing?

1204. Were quality procedures built into the Smart Machines project?

1205. How adequately involved did you feel in Smart Machines project decisions?

1206. How efficient were Smart Machines project team meetings conducted?

1207. How complete and timely were the materials you were provided to decide whether to proceed from one Smart Machines project lifecycle phase to the next?

1208. How closely did deliverables match what was defined within the Smart Machines project Scope?

1209. What things mattered the most on this Smart Machines project?

1210. Under what legal authority did your organization head and program manager direct your organization and Smart Machines project?

1211. How comprehensive was integration testing?

1212. How much flexibility is there in the funding (e.g., what authorities does the program manager have to change to the specifics of the funding within the overall funding ceiling)?

1213. How to write up the lesson identified – how will you document the results of your analysis corresponding that you have an li ready to take the next step in the ll process?

1214. How satisfied are you with your involvement in the development and/or review of the Smart Machines project Scope during Smart Machines project Initiation and Planning?

1215. Did the Smart Machines project change significantly?

1216. Was sufficient advance training conducted and/or information provided to enable the already stated affected by the changes to adjust to and accommodate them?

1217. How much of your time was spent on other than this Smart Machines project?

1218. How was the quality of products/processes assured?

1219. Was there a Smart Machines project Definition document. Was there a Smart Machines project Plan. Were they used during the Smart Machines project?

1220. Is there any way in which you think your development process hampered this Smart Machines project?

Index

remedial   41
remedies   38
remove   57
remunerate   66
repeat 191
repeatable   174
rephrased   11
report 5-6, 45, 75, 138, 152, 161, 177, 194, 218, 226, 237
reported   153, 166, 202, 222
reporting   77, 117, 146, 161, 188, 218, 220
reports 42, 107, 115, 117, 196
repository   184, 238
represent   59, 198-199, 230
reproduced   1
reputation   96
request   5, 48, 158, 184, 196-199
requested   1, 64, 186, 196, 198
requests   196-197
require 42, 70, 76, 130, 142, 233
required   17, 25, 30, 34, 63-64, 70, 103, 108, 129, 135-136,
148, 173, 180, 190-192, 207, 216-217, 225, 237
requiring   107, 234
research   21, 81, 138, 212
resemble   192
reserved   1
reserves   152
reside   154, 184
resilient 190
resolution   51, 123
resolve 136
resolved   150, 174, 231
resource   3-4, 115, 136, 142, 144-145, 147, 152, 170, 184,
195
resourced   202
resources   2, 9, 17, 27, 30, 45, 63, 65, 70, 73, 75, 79, 85, 90,
104, 110, 114, 123, 129, 135-137, 141, 145, 149, 155, 157-158, 170,
184, 188-189, 193, 205, 209, 216, 218, 236
respect   1
respond   110
responded   13
response   21-22, 71-73, 76-77, 190, 226
responsive   156
restrict 118

should 7, 17, 25, 31, 42, 49, 57, 61-62, 66, 71, 75, 81, 84, 87, 92, 97, 100, 103, 106-107, 111-113, 117, 126, 130, 134, 136, 138, 145, 166, 168-169, 174, 176, 178-179, 181-182, 186-187, 191, 196, 205-206, 212, 216, 230, 237
signature   90
signatures   142
signed 122, 224
signers 234
silent   207
similar 26-27, 48, 54, 60, 136, 154, 181
simple 92, 223
simply 9, 11
single   85, 207
single-use   7
situation   20, 35, 111, 154, 176, 222
skeptical   101
skills   20, 45, 91, 96, 138, 146, 167, 171, 177-178, 217-218, 224
slippage   180
smallest   19, 64
social   101, 182, 210
societal   97
software   18, 110, 114, 116-117, 125-126, 151, 174, 184, 192, 226-227
solicit   33, 208
soluiton   226
solution   37, 48, 51, 56-58, 60-63, 65, 68, 180, 226
solutions   42, 56, 60-61, 63-65
solving 210
someone   7, 233
someones   209
something   85, 112
Sometimes   42
sought 108
source 5, 90-91, 146, 154, 183, 186
sources   48, 51, 57, 79, 180, 208
special 73
specific   9, 21, 28-30, 49, 79, 126, 136, 139, 141-142, 144, 152, 154, 168, 171, 187, 194, 198, 219, 236
specifics   239
specified   98, 220, 232, 236
specify 202
Speech   119
spoken 91

```
sponsor        19, 115, 132, 147, 205, 228
sponsored      28
sponsors       18, 164, 206, 209
stability 40
stable  180
staffed 30
staffing 20, 72, 112
stages  189, 232
standard       7, 70, 133, 142, 170, 226-227
standards      1, 11-12, 69, 75, 104, 125-126, 160, 162, 165, 171,
189, 198, 225
started 9, 140
starting 12
start-up       206
stated  89, 93, 129, 160, 162, 224, 231, 239
statement      3, 12, 58, 62, 116, 122-123, 126, 155, 158
statements     13, 23, 29, 32, 34, 46-47, 55, 67, 77, 101, 117, 164
static   197
status  5-6, 53, 104, 152, 170, 175-176, 184, 188, 194, 222, 226
steering       152
storage        219
strategic      73, 92, 177, 212, 224-225
strategies     90, 94, 110, 200-202
strategy       22, 56, 70, 85, 87, 97, 114, 132, 170, 172, 200
strengths      138, 229
strictly  233
strong  146
stronger       98
Strongly       12, 17, 24, 35, 47, 56, 68, 78, 197
structure      3, 65, 92, 98, 122, 127, 144, 152, 171, 180-181, 203
stubborn       85
stupid  86
styles   160
subdivided     129
subfactor      187
subject 9-10, 25
Subjective     117, 163
submit  11
submitted      11, 198-199
subset  19
sub-teams      212
succeed        87
```

277